REMEMBER THE LORD:
The Musings of St. Peter's Wife

D. Algernon Laity

May God richly bless you
as you read!

David Laity

Author Contact Information:

David Laity
116 – 1450 Bertram St.
Kelowna, B.C., Canada V1Y 8R9
dtlaity57@gmail.com

Acknowledgments:

To my wife, Teresa, who continually encouraged me to write and publish this book.

To the Sweetnams and my niece, Marilyn who gave much needed advice in getting started with publication.

To all the teachers and professors who taught me history throughout my life. Especially to Dr. Susie Stanley who strengthened my love of history and had me as her Teaching Assistant.

For all those who have put up with my ramblings concerning history in conversations with them.

CONTENTS

Prologue

"So my darling Peter, we will finally be separated in this life, but it won"t be long before we are together again forever. Little did I think that I would precede you in seeing our Lord once more. It is fitting that your last words to me as I passed by your cell to be taken out to be martyred should be, "Remember the Lord". Those words are such an encouragement and comfort to me at this time as I am sure they are to you as well. Waiting for my final end gives me time to ponder our life together and our relationship with our Lord. I know that you can not hear me as you are in another part of this prison but I will imagine that we are together much like those evenings in the past when we would go over what each of us had experienced that day. We did our best to have those times together even when we had our daughter. I remember how we would put her to bed and wait for her to fall asleep so that we would have uninterrupted time to talk. I loved that time so much, being alone with you and sharing my heart with you.

I could not always call Jesus "Lord". My thoughts about the man and his being "Lord" have changed over the years. I have had my questions and doubts as my emotions went up and down over those three short years that we were with him. Since our first meeting I have considered Him as "Lord" in different ways. First I saw him as a local "rabbi" or religious teacher, then as a major religious leader.

At times I even thought that he might possibly become "lord" as king of our nation. I now accept him as the true "LORD", creator and owner of all things and demanding of complete honour and obedience.

I am being taken to the Tullianum, that final holding cell, where I will be kept along with other prisoners awaiting their imminent deaths. I suppose I will have enough time in that place to remember my journey in coming to know Jesus as our Lord. In spite of your knowing that I will soon face the executioner's sword, I realize that you can rejoice even now in the fact that I am being called home.

ONE

Galilee: My Childhood Home

Home - what a wonderful word! You and I are going
to our heavenly home that our Lord has prepared for us. "A
mansion.", he said. I can hardly imagine what it will be like
but I shall soon know it in full. I will see it first hand not just
through spiritual eyes and it will be our home for all eternity.

In this world there have been a number of places that
we have called home. Each has had its own special
attractions and memories. They have been places of love,
family, friends, hopes and dreams. Each has had its own
unique events. Rome, has never felt like home to me even
with all the other brothers and sisters around us here,
including the revered brother Paul. It isn't that the city is so
large but that it is so imperial, so full of affluence, sensuality,
pomp and cruelty. The Empire was founded on immorality
and violence and it has continued building on that same
foundation to this day. I hate the gladiatorial games where
cheers go up for the deaths of innocent people and even of
dumb beasts. The saddest of all is when our own brothers
and sisters in Christ are placed into the arena for sport. The
audience jeers as the brothers and sisters do not cry out to be
spared, nor fight back, nor curse but simply pray for those
who abuse them and then sing praises to the Lord. I do not

3

know how those believers that live in the very palace of Caesar can bear it. While Nero is a brute, our Lord would have him repent so not to perish. But for now it is he who will send us to our deaths. Yet we are the victors, as brother Paul says, "to be absent from the body is to be present with the Lord."

Of all of the places that I have called home over the years the one that is dearest to me is Capernaum, "village of consolation or comfort", in the province of Galilee. Place of my birth and early years, it has always been a comfort to me.

Ah, Galilee! When I was a child I believed that this must have been the area where our first parents, Adam and Eve, were originally formed and first lived, that Paradise, the Garden of Eden. Galilee, land of a hundred hills interspersed with numerous small green plains. Well-watered by ample rains and many small springs, groves of trees sprung up as did many small villages. I particularly loved the groves of mimosa, jasmine and oleander with their beautiful flowers and sweet fragrances. Each village being surrounded by fertile soil established its own cluster of well laid out fields. I shall never forget the beauty of the golden grain in sharp contrast with the vibrant blue flowers of the fields of flax. As a girl I chased butterflies in those fields and often received a scolding from the owners when I happened to flatten some of their crops. As I would wander further from the village I would come upon the uncultivated land where oceans of wildflowers and flowering trees filled the countryside. The villages had vineyards and orchards. Fruit and nuts were in abundance -- figs, olives, pomegranates, oranges, walnuts and dates. The grapes and figs supplied fruit for ten months of the year while different plants produced their crops during the other two months.

One can not get the complete picture of the Galilee

without a description of the lake that it bordered. We Galileans called it the Sea of Galilee but that was certainly an exaggerated title to use when describing a body of water that a boat under normal sail could cross in half an hour. It was more aptly called the Lake of Gennesaret because of its harp-like shape. As proud Jews we disdained to call it the Lake of Tiberius, the name that Herod Antipas gave to it in honour of the hated Emperor of Rome, Tiberius Claudius Nero.

No matter how it was named the lake was beautiful with its deep clear water. Its colouring varied from blues to greens with the occasional reds. Particularly breath taking were its reflections of early morning sunrises and late evening sunsets. Although the lake presented the dangers of fierce winds and threats of violent fevers to those who visited the area, we scarcely thought of those possibilities when we strolled along its magnificent shores caught up in its picturesque grandeur.

Galilee, so different from Judea, that dry and colourless province in the south. That part of our nation had sparse vegetation and areas of desert. It is better known for its rocks than for its crops. Judea, rigid and austere like its people, a land of shepherds and of priests. The people of Galilee were so different, softer in spirit though still rugged, especially its fishermen. Galileans were an easier going people than the Judeans, not so strict in observing the law yet still deeply religious. Though we could be quarrelsome and disobliging at times, we were generally known for being charitable, helping the old, the poor and the needy.

Galileans were looked down on by the religious elite of Jerusalem. Our particular dialect and faulty pronunciation of many of the Hebrew words even prompted the religious leaders to ban us from acting as readers of public prayers. They called us the *am - ha - arez*, "people of the earth". And so we, the hard working, fun loving Galileans, would prove to be the first to be open to the "earthy" gospel that our Lord would preach. One of the things that first attracted us to Jesus was his use of stories about the things that we were familiar with -- the mustard seed, lilies, sowing and reaping, the birds of the field, vineyards and sheep folds. His message spoke of the everyday matters of life.

This crowded Roman cell in which I now sit reminds me in some ways of our house in Capernaum when it was packed with the poor and sick pressing in to see our Lord. In those days everyone knew it as your house, Peter, but in reality it was my house, or should I say my mother's house. My father had built it when he was engaged to my mother. As you know my father was a stone mason so he built a good house, one meant to last. It was the house that I grew up in as an only child and it was never so full as when Jesus came into our lives. But I am getting ahead of myself.

Since my father belonged to the same guild as the other tradesmen in the area our house was situated on the same street as the other builders . It fronted a large common courtyard and it was there during the warm season that we often cooked and ate together and had such happy times with the families that dwelt in the other homes around that square. I particularly enjoyed the times after supper in the early evening when the families would gather together in the courtyard to talk. The men would mainly discuss their work or the latest taxes the Romans had instituted while the women talked about their families and the plans that they had for their children. I enjoyed hearing the chatter and frequent laughter. I loved to feel the breeze off the lake and to watch the fires flicker as the night wore on. Many were the times that I would fall asleep in the courtyard and my parents would have to carry me inside to my bed.

Our house was only a short distance from the lake and close to the synagogue. Since my father was one of the ten adult males required for the forming of a synagogue, he had responsibilities for its upkeep. The residents of our town were all so proud of having their own synagogue and not having to travel to some larger town for worship and teaching. A Roman centurion had had it built out of black basalt. This man must have been one of those God seeking gentiles that we called "God - fearers". It would be in our synagogue that our Lord would teach and even cast out an evil spirit from a man. It was after he fed the five thousand with five barley loaves and two small fishes that he entered our synagogue and declared himself to be the "bread of life" and that anyone who would come to him and believe in him would never go hungry or be thirsty. At that time I was amazed and puzzled by his actions and words and even felt a little fearful.

But back to our house. It was fairly large for our town since father could get all the materials and do most of the work himself. Other than its large size it was like most other houses in town. It consisted of one large room. In that room we lived on a raised platform away from the door. During the cold times we cooked indoors and even brought in some of the animals in order to add some much appreciated warmth. Of course these animals were kept close to the door. Having a fire indoors without a proper chimney filled the house with smoke so we cooked our meals as quickly as possible. Under the platform we would store our tools and clay storage jars in which we kept our food supplies such as flour, oil and dried fish. Our cooking utensils and bed clothes were kept on top of the platform along with the thin wool filled mattresses for us to sleep on and a straw mat where our dishes full of food would be placed as we reclined on the

floor to eat our meals. At night I enjoyed laying on my
sleeping mattress and playing games with my mother by the
light of our terracotta lamp which burned olive oil and gave
off a dim, smoky light from its flax wick.

I especially loved the rooftop of our house that was
accessed by stairs outside of the house itself. It was a place
to get away, where secrets could be whispered and
announcements shouted. I liked to lie on the rooftop at night
and view all the stars that filled the sky. I would think of the
words that our father David, shepherd boy and king, had
written in one of his psalms. "The heavens declare the glory
of God." Everything in this world pointed to our God, its
creator. It was on the rooftop that we would erect our booth
for Succoth festival. Eating and sleeping there we
remembered our God's provision for our ancestors as they
dwelt in the wilderness for forty years. Another thing that I
liked about our rooftop was that if I needed to get to some
other part of town quickly I could just jump from roof to
neighbouring roof and descend the stairs of the house closest
to my destination. By doing this I avoided the hustle and
bustle of the dusty, crowded, narrow streets of our town.

It was on the rooftops that the families would build
the guestroom, where guests would have their own entrance
and not be disturbed by the rest of the family. Father built a
splendid guest room and loved to have guests over just to
show it off. It was this room that our Lord would often use
during his ministry in Galilee. Father never did see our Lord
as he died of fever shortly before Jesus came into our lives. I
often smile when I think of what father would have done if he
had been there when the paralytic's friends tore up our roof to
get him to Jesus. But again my thoughts stray.

Much of my childhood was spent working around the
house. Cleaning, carrying water from the village well,

tending the herb garden and helping to prepare meals. Mother loved to cook and enjoyed teaching me to cook also. I must admit that I learned quite well from her and over the years I have had many a comment on my culinary skills. Of course I never had to worry about what I would feed you, Peter. You would eat anything that I set before you. I also helped to care for the lamb that we would raise for the Passover sacrifice and I inevitably became quickly attached to it. I always cried when father would take the lamb to the temple to be slaughtered even though I realized the importance of that sacrifice as taught by my father and mother at each Seder meal during Passover. I also had other animals to care for, some chickens, a few doves, a donkey and our cow. But these were never as dear to me as the Pascal lamb. From time to time I made pets of some of the other animals and even fashioned small replicas of them out of clay.

As a child I always enjoyed learning new things, especially those relating to our religion. The rabbis did not approve of girls getting as much education as the boys and women were not allowed to teach in the synagogues since the rabbis thought that women were "of a lighter mind". Not having any brothers I wanted to make my parents proud of me by being the equal to any boy in our village. My father who held strongly to our traditions was not pleased by this. Our education always revolved around our religion since it was more than just a creed to us but a way of life. In fact it was our life. Learning was centered on the study of the Scriptures which we believed came directly from God, especially the first five books known as the Torah, the "law" or "teaching". We were taught that the law was written on the tablets of stone by the very finger of God. Our many feasts also taught us so much as father would explain to us the significance of each one as we celebrated it.

I remember my mother teaching me the alphabet at the age of three and then the Scriptures at the age of five. We didn't begin with the Psalms or historical books but with the book of Leviticus, so that we would know the law of our God early in life. While the boys of the town began school in the synagogue at the age of six I continued my education at home. The desired qualities for women were meekness, modesty and shamefacedness not learning and intelligence. I strove for both. I excelled in whatever I studied because of my great desire for knowledge. I read the Scriptures and asked questions of all who would give me a hearing. I looked forward to our religious feasts with all their history and ceremony. There was a hallowed sanctity about them that was only for us, God's chosen people. And there were so many more people at these feasts that I could talk with and learn from.

When I had some free time I enjoyed playing games with the other children in the village. These games were often played with dice, balls and even simple stones. I particularly liked the children's circle dances and the jumping games. But there was very little time for games with all the chores and times set aside for education . I often wished that I would have had brothers and sisters to share the load. This made me even more grateful for the weekly Sabbath as it was a day of sacred rest and a joy to be shared by all.

Peter, I still remember that day when we first met. I was twelve years old, having just come of age and I had gone with father to the lake-shore to buy some fish. Your father would bring some of his fish from your home town of Bethsaida, which meant "House of Fish", to sell in our town of Capernaum. My father chose your father, Jonas, to purchase his fish from because of his reputation for honesty and for his wide variety of fresh fish. He also chose your father because he knew that he had two fine young sons working with him, one of which could possibly become a husband for me and a son-in-law for him. My father preferred Andrew but that day Jonas gave the fish that father had paid for to you to give to me. I remember how I blushed as you handed me the three small tilapia. You smiled gently and then gave out such a boisterous laugh. I ran home embarrassed but that smile and laugh always remained with me. It wasn't your rugged and handsome looks but that smile and laugh that attracted me to you. I know that my father had already had plans of arranging a marriage with the family of Jonas, but I believe that that encounter solidified that decision in his mind. He then realized that it would be you, and not your brother, that was ordained by God for me.

TWO

Marriage

After our first meeting, Peter, our fathers quickly set
their plans in motion. They began to negotiate the "mohar",
the bride price. Our marriage was not an agreement between
you and myself but between our two families. It was your
father that had to take on all the expenses of the marriage.
Since I was an only child, father wanted a good price as he
realized that my mother would be losing my valuable help
around the house. And father did get a good price from your
father both in coin and in goods. And I also was to receive
the "mattan", those gifts from you, the prospective groom. I
remember the fine clothing and jewels that you gave me.
Also my father gave me a portion of his fields to bring into
our marriage. Your father was not only an honest man but a
generous one. He added one of his fishing boats to the gifts
so that you would be set up in your own business. Everyone
was happy when the negotiations were completed and the
"calling of the damsel and inquiring of her mouth" took
place. That is when I, as our custom demanded, accepted our
fathers' choice of you to be my husband. But Peter, this was
not a mere formality in my case because I had truly loved you

from that very first meeting. And I love you even more now. I still remember the benediction that was pronounced as we drank the cup of wine symbolizing the covenant relation we were entering into. "Blessed are You, O Lord, our God, King of the universe, who has sanctified us with Your commandments and given us commandments concerning forbidden sexual relations, and has forbidden any sexual relations to those who are merely betrothed, and permitted them to those lawfully married by covenant. Blessed are you, O Lord, who sanctifies your people by covenant." You then gave me some coins which sealed the betrothal. From that point on I was sanctified, set apart, exclusively for you.

With the negotiations completed we entered into the betrothal period of our marriage. You returned to your father's house and although we were considered as good as married I remained with my parents for over a year. During that time I was careful to follow our custom of wearing a veil whenever I left the house. This custom dictated that no one outside of my immediate family would see my face until after the wedding feast was concluded.

You had gone to your father's house in Bethsaida to prepare our accommodations and I began to prepare for married life. Mother had already started teaching me many things such as cooking, cleaning, sewing and the smooth running of a Jewish household along with the preparations of the many yearly feasts. Now she began to teach me the finer things of marriage, the art of pleasing a husband. She taught the art of quickly recognizing a husband's likes and dislikes and how to capitalize on knowing these things. She went over the importance of preparing his meals on time and of keeping his clothes clean and mended. Although I was young, mother went over the area of pleasing one's husband in the bedroom. Though I blushed at the time, I paid close attention as I already knew that this was an important part of marriage. Mother always used the Scripture in her teaching. She went over the Song of Solomon, that beautiful poem concerning married love. She also used the great passage found in the book of Proverbs about a virtuous woman. It is that portion of Scripture that all noble Jewish women try to emulate in their marriages. Above all my mother taught me by example. She loved my father and I knew it. I believe that you too, Peter, saw that and were thinking of my mother when you penned those words to wives in your letter to the churches. I think that you were especially thinking of her when you wrote that beauty should not come from outward adornment but it should come from the inner self, the beauty of a gentle and quiet spirit which would never fade and would be of great worth in God's sight.

As the year of separation drew to a close my anticipation of our marriage day grew. I knew that your coming would be soon but I did not know the precise day or time of that coming. This reminds me of what our Lord said of his own coming; that no one would know the day or the hour. As each day passed I prepared myself more and more. I knew that the coming was usually at night and would be preceded by a shout so that the bride would be forewarned in order to be ready to leave quickly with the groom. Each night I would lay out my wedding dress and the precious stones and jewels that I would wear for our wedding. Many of those ornaments had been passed down from generation to generation. Our family was well off so we didn't have to borrow anything to wear from our friends as many of the poorer families in our village had to. Also golden ornaments and pearls were braided into my long raven hair. I shall never forget all the preparation that went into getting ready for your coming. As the prophet Jeremiah wrote, "Can a maid forget her ornaments, or a bride her attire?" I know that I shall never forget mine. I believe that "memory" is just one proof of eternity. When I think of my time of preparation I think of how the church should be preparing itself for the coming of our Lord. Many were the nights that I awoke to what I thought was "the shout" only to be disappointed to find out that it was the wail of some drunken reveler or the cry of some jackal or other wild animal. So the time seemed to drag on.

Finally that greatly anticipated night came and the shout was given and you arrived with your best man and other male escorts. This time I knew that the shout was the real thing and I gathered my female attendants together. I can still picture you dressed in your best apparel trying to appear as much as a king as possible. You couldn't afford a golden crown so you wore a garland of fresh flowers as a substitute. I remember your garments being scented with frankincense and myrrh. And so began the torchlight procession from my home to your father's house where you had prepared our new abode. And what a procession that was as the wedding party danced and sang in the flickering glow of the torches to the music played on flutes, lyres, tambourines and drums. When we arrived at your father's house there was a great gathering of family and friends to welcome us. Many of these had traveled great distances from various parts of Israel. Some even came from the holy city of Jerusalem.

After the initial greetings I remember being escorted by the wedding company to the "huppah" or bridal chamber. From the time I had left my father's house I had been veiled as required by our ancient custom so that no one could see my face. I couldn't help but think of the story of my two ancestors, Rachel and Leah, and the deception played on Jacob. But, Peter, there was no fear of you receiving the wrong bride. We entered the bridal chamber alone while the rest of the party waited outside and there in the privacy of that chamber we consummated our marriage thus fulfilling the covenant that had been made just over a year earlier. This was the first time that we had "known" each other and we fulfilled God's plan as found in the Pentateuch where it was said to the very first man and woman that a man was to leave his parents and be joined to his wife and become one flesh.

After some time together you alone left the bridal chamber with great joy to announce the consummation of our marriage to those waiting outside. From inside the bridal chamber I heard the shouts and laughter that went up as the announcement was concluded. Those who had been waiting quickly passed on the news of our union to the rest of the wedding guests. A great shout went up as the news was announced to the crowd and such merriment followed. I wasn't embarrassed in the least when they announced the consummation of our marriage as some might think for this had been our custom for centuries and mother had shared all of the details with me during the time of preparation. The traditional feasting began and the merriment lasted for seven days, the period we called "the seven days of the huppah". During this time I remained shut away in the bridal chamber while you and the wedding guests feasted on lamb stewed with barley, bread, sardines, endive, raisins, dates, candied almonds and fresh fruit. And of course there was plenty of Galilean red wine. Most of all you enjoyed each others' company. I could hear all the merriment from our room when in the evenings the guests squatted around various small fires telling and listening to stories, pondering over riddles or enjoying musical recitals. I resented not being present at the festivities a little but I resigned myself to our sacred traditions and looked forward to the times in the future that you and I would be able to celebrate others' weddings together. At the end of "the seven days of huppah" you, Peter, brought me out of the bridal chamber unveiled so that all could see who your bride was and I shall never forget the look of pride and love that I saw in your eyes that day.

THREE

A Fisherman's Wife

I began my life in our new home and was no longer known as the stone mason's daughter but as the fisherman's wife. You had prepared such a lovely house connected to your father's home. As I busied myself putting my things around the house and giving it a woman's touch, little did I realize that our time there would be short. For within the first year of our marriage my father died of fever and my mother took ill as well. We decided to move in with my mother and from then on father's fine stone mason's house became known as your house, the house of Simeon the fisherman. Your brother took over our own little house in Bethsaida but when years later you joined up with the Rabbi he moved in with us. At this time our home became the headquarters for our Lord's ministry.

I remember those ten years we had together before you left to follow the Rabbi. You and your brother were successful fishermen and I was a contented, fisherman's wife. It seems so long ago and it is hard to remember that you were called Simeon at that time. Simeon meant "hearing" and you would soon hear the voice of the Lord.

Life in Capernaum was good. Although some thought that Capernaum meant "Town of Nahum", it apparently had no connection with our famed prophet of that name. It was only a small village but an important one as it was situated on the famous Via Maris, "Way of the Sea", the Roman road that ran from the Mediterranean to Damascus. Being situated on this road we were introduced to many different cultures as we met the travelers from all parts of the Roman Empire. We were also introduced to many different trade goods including the coveted silks and spices from the far east. It was a joy to get to see all those fine things. But being situated on that road was a detriment to our own culture as we were introduced to various foreign religions, customs and ever increasing materialism. Many of our own people began to desire the new things that they were being introduced to and some of our people even strayed from the holiness found in our own true faith.

Our town was in the tetrarchy of Galilee that after the death of Herod the Great was ruled by his son, that "old fox", Herod Antipas. It was also very close to the tetrarchy of Gaulantis which was to the east of us and ruled by Antipas's brother, Herod Philip. Being near the border of these two tetrarchies and on the main trade route between east and west, we had our own customs house run by those hated tax collectors known as publicans. These men were despised by the local population because while they were Galileans, like us, they were in the direct pay of rich Roman officials. They also tended to be greedy and corrupt. The publicans would examine the goods passing through our town, value them and then write out tariff tickets and enforce their payment. They also collected the regular taxes designated for the running of the Roman empire. All the payments were sent to Rome. This tax and tariff system fostered the overcharging of taxes

19

and the laying of false charges by the publicans of smuggling in the hope of gaining a bribe. It is little wonder that people would often view the presence of Matthew, a former tax collector, among our Lord's disciples with question, suspicion and even contempt.

Capernaum's position on the Via Maris also made it a prime place to have a Roman military post since the closest Roman garrison was at Tiberias, some sixteen kilometers away. So Roman soldiers settled just east of our village. While these troops provided a sense of security, especially against thieves they also presented the vices of gambling, drunkenness, public bathing and prostitution. Added to these evils were the times that soldiers would force hard labour upon our men and sexual favours from our women. I often wondered how God could allow these things to happen in His land.

Being on the trade route was good for us economically as we had easy access to selling and exporting our goods, especially our fish. Fish was the most commonly eaten meat throughout our nation, then chicken was next in popularity. Beef and lamb were served only on special occasions like the religious feasts and weddings. For us as Jews pork and crustaceans were strictly forbidden. Since you, Peter, were a fisherman we had a steady income and wanted for nothing. And we always had plenty of food. Although fishermen were often looked down on as being ignorant men, that was not the truth. In reality fishermen were experienced, multilingual businessmen being fluent in their native Aramaic as well as being conversant in Hebrew which was the language of our religion, Greek the universal language of trade and business, and even some Latin, that hated political language of the Empire. No wonder our Lord chose so many fishermen as disciples.

As well as needing to be skilled in the arts of fishing and sailing, fishermen needed to be adept at boat building, sail making and net mending. They also had to be quick judges of personal character especially when dealing with the trade merchants. Fishermen even needed a general knowledge of accounting, law, religion and civil duty. As I got to know more of the fishermen, I found them to be, on the whole, patient, optimistic, community minded and above all strong and hard working.

I could tell that you loved your work, except for the times when you didn't catch anything. Times, I might add, that were few and far between. You had a pride in your ability to read the signs for where the fish would be at any given time and for what type of net you should use. I particularly liked to watch you as you threw out the cast net from your boat. You certainly needed perfect balance to do this and it seemed like magic as the net went above your head and out over the water in a perfect circle encompassing a whole school of fish. Then you would draw the fish in with your muscles straining especially when you had a particularly large catch.

The other types of nets you used were not as interesting to watch. There was the dragnet which was the oldest method of fishing used in your trade. This method needed another boat and crew to accomplish its task. That is why you and your brother teamed up with James and John, the sons of Zebedee. The heavy dragnet, up to 300 feet long and 12 feet deep, would be loaded onto one boat with one end of it being held on shore by the crew of the boat that would remain on the bank. The net was dropped into the water and a half circle was formed as the boat returned to shore. Then the crews of both boats would drag the catch onto land.

The trammel net had three layers of netting of

different sizes of mesh which enabled it to catch all types and sizes of fish. Fishing with this type of net was usually done at night and had to be done in deep water so that the fine meshed nets would not be torn on any rocks. When we needed a few extra fish for the times that guests dropped in unannounced, you generally used hook and line. I still remember the time that you caught that one large fish with your bare hands! How proud you looked as you held it up and made out as if it was nothing out of the ordinary.

Fishing certainly produced strong healthy bodies along with strong healthy appetites. This kept me busy grinding grain to make those fresh loaves that you used to enjoy along with the fresh fish that you would bring home.

I also enjoyed watching you and the other fishermen sort the catch once it was brought in. You were so skillful in distinguishing between the different species. And there were so many types found in our little Gennesaret. Someone once told me that our God had blessed our small land with some forty-five different species of fish and that eighteen of those were common to Galilee. First the fish had to be sorted into clean and unclean according to our religious law. The unclean, those without scales, like catfish and eel would be sold to the Gentiles. Of the clean fish, I particularly liked the common musht or talapia. This was the type of fish that you caught with a coin in its mouth. You were not terribly surprised to find the coin as you thought that the fish had simply picked it up while gathering rocks to fill its mouth. These fish regularly do this to keep their offspring from continuing to use their mouths for refuge from predators. Pebbles in the adult fish's mouth would let the fry know that they were big enough to be on their own. So some didn't view the finding of the coin as a real miracle. I even think that you had your doubts but I always thought it was one. It was a miracle that you would catch that particular fish just at that precise time and that the coin you found would be the exact coin, a full silver shekel, needed to pay the temple tax for both you and our Lord. The sorting of the fish had to be done quickly since by law fish to be sold as "fresh" would have to still have the water on them. That is why the locals would come down to the shore as soon as they saw the boats begin to come in.

Fish were not only eaten fresh. In fact most were salted or dried to preserve them and keep them for export. The dried fish from Galilee were considered a delicacy especially by the aristocracy of Rome and Damascus. There was also the manufacture of "garum", a fish sauce relished throughout the Empire. This sauce was made from the smaller fish, the sardines, smelts, small mullets and sprats or anchovies, to which was added the entrails of the larger fish. A vat of this mixture would be allowed to sit in the hot sun until it was "aged" and then it would be strained, bottled and sold throughout the Empire. It was often mixed with wine and used as seasoning on all sorts of other foods. Magdala, the home town of Mary from whom our Lord cast out the demons, was a major center for the production of garum and was nicknamed Tarichaeae meaning Processed-Fish Village. You could always know when you were nearing this town just from the delightful aroma that would greet you well before you could see the town itself. Spain claimed to produce the best garum but those in the Galilee felt that Galilean garum was equal to, if not better than, the Spanish product. You, Peter, had such a liking for garum that I remember commenting to you one time when you were not listening to me that I should use some of the sauce as perfume in order to get your attention.

After sorting the fish came the arduous task of

mending the nets. The nets were made from flax, as were the sails, and could be easily broken and needed much attention after each outing. I remember that you took the task of caring for them yourself rather than hiring labourers to do so as most of the other fishermen would. You always felt that no one else could do a good enough job. First the holes in the nets caused by rocks, logs, and sometimes by the fish themselves needed to be mended. Then the nets needed to be washed, dried and folded to be ready for the next trip.

With all this work to do we had little time together. I spent most of my time working around the home and in caring for the few goats, sheep and chickens that we had and in tending our own little garden. I enjoyed milking the goats as these animals almost became pets with each one having its own unique personality. I love one story found in the Scriptures written by the prophet Samuel. This was the account of how Nathan the prophet related to King David about a poor man who only had one little pet lamb that he loved and treated as if it were his own daughter. He fed it from his table and let it drink from his own cup and it even slept in his arms. And there was a rich and powerful man who took the poor man's lamb for sacrifice even though he had many sheep of his own. I have often thought about that story and imagined the sorrow, anger and injustice that the poor man and his family must have felt.

In our garden we grew onions and garlic along with many of the herbs that I used in my cooking -- cumin, coriander, mint, dill and mustard. I took pride in the soups and stews that I would prepare for you using just the right combinations of the herbs that I had grown myself.

My work became more difficult when I became pregnant but mother was a great help. I hadn't allowed her to do much before since I felt there could only be one mistress of the house. But now I needed the help. I had lost children during childbirth before and didn't want to lose this one. We had often felt that God was displeased with us for some reason and I remember how happy we were when our daughter was born. I saw the pride on your face on that day although I detected some disappointment that she was not a boy. Little did we know then that she would be our only child just as I had been the only child for my parents. We named her Martha, meaning "lady", for our desire for her was to grow into a fine virtuous young lady. At that time we never dreamed that she would more commonly be known by a nickname taken from your own changed name. She would be known as Petronella. This was not because she looked like you, as thankfully she resembled me, but because she had inherited your strong, impetuous disposition.

So our lives went on day in and day out with little change. We were happy, you with your fishing and I with the care of our home and of our daughter. But a drastic change would soon come. You would meet our Lord.

FOUR

First Encounters with Jesus

We were happily living our lives centered around the
raising our little daughter. She was our joy. And then came
the day that was to start the process that would prove to
change our lives for ever. That was the day that your brother,
Andrew, came running to our house shouting, "We have
found the Messiah! We have found the Messiah! His name
is Jesus!" I had never seen Andrew so excited before and you
too caught that excitement. You left your supper on the table
and immediately went with your brother to Bethabara across
the Jordan from Jericho to meet this man, Jesus. I was
somewhat upset as you left not even touching the meal that I
had painstakingly prepared. I didn't understand at the time
what all the fuss was about in finding the Messiah. There
were often reports in our country of someone claiming to be
the Messiah. But this time things seemed different some
how.

Andrew had always been inquisitive about spiritual
things. He was a quiet and sensitive man. He wasn't
religious in the traditional, ceremonial way but he did take his
quest for God seriously. He internalized his religion and was
always looking for some mystical revelation as he read the

Scriptures. That is why he had become a disciple of John, that strange, rough and boisterous man who was nicknamed "The Baptist".

I remember how you would be upset when Andrew would take days off from fishing to be with this man and how you would complain to him when he would return. Andrew would tell you of how John was a prophet and how he had studied with the mystic Jewish sect, the Essenes, in that Messianic community at Qumran near the Dead Sea. He also told you of how John had left that group and dressed himself in camel skins, eating grasshoppers and honey as he preached repentance throughout the wilderness areas of the Jordan valley. He declared that he was preparing the way for the coming of the Messiah and many were attracted to him. Large numbers of people came from the cities and villages to hear him. Even some of the religious leaders from Jerusalem came to see him.

I remember how I used to wonder whatever attracted gentle Andrew to John. I always thought that it would be you that would go in for that sort of person. You were more of a practical hands on type of man and had always wanted to see the benefits that religion could give to the events of everyday life. So I guess that is why you went with your brother that day. Andrew told you how John, The Baptist, had called this Jesus the Lamb of God. You wanted to judge the man for yourself.

I remember you coming home from your trip to Bethabara. You were so full of questions. You told me that when you met Jesus the first thing that he had said to you was that your name would be changed from Simeon to Cephas or Peter, meaning a "small stone". Knowing that the giving of names was important in our culture you wondered what this changing of your name meant. This interested you and you wanted to learn more. You were excited when Jesus decided to visit the Galilee and began gathering disciples along the way. He found Philip who introduced him to his friend Nathanael and they too decided to follow Jesus and learn more. All were so desiring the coming of the Messiah to rid them of the hated Romans and their hopes were beginning to grow with the emergence of this new Rabbi.

One day after Jesus arrived in Galilee there was a wedding in Cana and he and those with him were invited to attend. The bride was a cousin of mine and we too had been invited to the wedding. Since your brother was going with Jesus's group we decided to travel with them. Not only would this help us get to know Jesus better it would provide protection from any bandits along the way. I must say that this made me feel a lot safer and I could also enjoy the company of some of the other women traveling with us. Little did we imagine what was about to happen at Cana.

The wedding feast was like any other Jewish wedding feast and brought back memories of our own wedding. I could just imagine the excitement of our cousin and the concern of the planners that everything would go smoothly. No one would foresee any problem arising as our ceremonies had been the same for centuries. But someone slipped up somewhere. Possibly they underestimated the number of guests that would attend or the heightened thirst that the guests would have due to the intense heat of the day. Needless to say there was a great concern and embarrassment when the supply of wine ran out. Jesus' mother was there and being one who wanted to fix things went to her son and told him about the situation. At first it seemed that Jesus didn't really care but shortly after we came to see that that wasn't true. He truly was concerned and called the servants and told them to fill up six large, stone water pots used for religious cleansing with water. When they had filled them he commanded them to draw out some of the water and take it to the attendant in charge of the feast. We had to give those servants credit for obeying Jesus's instructions as they would surely be punished for bringing water instead of wine. But Jesus always spoke with authority. What amazement when what they poured out of the jugs was wine. We had all seen those jugs filled with water. How could the water in those pots have been turned into wine? Was this magic or some kind of sorcery? And the wine wasn't cheap wine but it was top quality wine as if it had been aged for years. The attendant was not only amazed at the water being turned into wine but as to its quality. The normal practice was to serve poor quality wine near the end of the festivities since by that time most of the guests couldn't tell the difference anyway. But this wine was top grade. Our Lord always did things well.

Peter, I don't know what your thoughts were at that time but mine were as to how Jesus had performed that trick. Most saw this as a miracle. Later we would come to learn that this was, in fact, the first miracle ever done by Jesus. Well, because of this miracle many believed in Jesus and a seed of faith was planted within you. Yet we returned home and you went back to your fishing.

I remember that for days after our return things were quiet in our house as both you and I pondered over what we had experienced at the wedding and from just being with this new rabbi. Even our daughter, Martha, was quiet as she sensed that her parents were deeply affected by something. Was this man just another prophet? Was he the one that would come as prophesied in the Scriptures? Was he the Messiah? We went over and over that first miracle in our minds. Was it really a miracle or some kind of trick or

magic? Others had claimed to do miracles in the past. Even
our own prophets like Elijah and Elisha had done miracles by
the power of God. Was this new rabbi a true prophet of God
or the Messiah or was he some charlatan or deluded person?
We had heard the rumours of his being the illegitimate son of
a carpenter from the small insignificant village of Nazareth.
Even our own people wondered at times if anything good,
especially a prophet of God, could come from Nazareth. But
at least he was a Galilean. Again we heard rumours of how at
the early age of twelve this Jesus had confounded the priests
when his family had visited the temple in Jerusalem during
Passover. What was the truth about this man? You and I
would discuss this over and over. At times we would think he
was just a man and other times we would think that he truly
could be the Messiah. Soon we would come to think that he
was much more than either of these.

So Peter, you heard more and more news about Jesus
from his followers. Now and then you took some time off
from your fishing to go and see for yourself what was
happening, but only for short periods of time. Then came
that day which became a turning point in your life or should I
say our lives? Jesus had come to Capernaum to teach and
one day he came upon you and Andrew fishing on the lake.
Jesus shouted out to you to come and be one of his disciples
and he would teach you how to fish for men. He always
knew how to use examples that would interest his hearers and
that had just enough mystery in them to cause people to
become inquisitive. Well this certainly got your attention and
both you and Andrew immediately left your nets and
followed him. This scene replayed itself a little ways down
the shore but this time with James and John. They too left
their boat and their father to follow Jesus. I wonder what
their father thought as he was left there all alone with the

fishing boat.

I know the questions that I had when later you all showed up at our house to tell us the news that you would be leaving your fishing for quite some time in order to go with Jesus. First I thought that you were joking. Then when I saw that you were serious I was afraid. What would our daughter and I do? How would we make ends meet? Would we have to depend on our family and friends to provide for us or would we get other fishermen to use our boat and then collect monies from them? How long would this last?

Whatever possessed you to make such an important decision so quickly and without consulting me first? Could it have been that time a few days earlier when you had toiled all night but caught nothing that had influenced you? I remember that while you were cleaning your nets the next morning Jesus came along and asked to use your boat in order to preach to the crowds along the shore. Jesus entered your boat and you pushed it some distance into the water. Everyone could hear the teaching as Jesus spoke. As you know, sound travels so well over water. Well, when he had finished speaking he asked you to cast out your net. You tried to explain to him that this would be futile since you had fished all night and caught nothing but Jesus's authority seemed to compel you to obey. As you halfheartedly put out the net over the side of the boat we all saw the fish appear from nowhere and fill the net. Some even seemed to jump into the net from outside of it. There were so many fish that we feared that the net would break so James and John came alongside with their boat to help. Was this a miracle or just coincidence?

But my fears about your decision to leave your fishing to follow Jesus seemed to flee and a real peace came into my heart when he told me not to worry as his father would provide. How could his father provide? Hadn't he died some years back? Was there an inheritance? Certainly this man had a powerful, commanding yet comforting way about him. This would prove not to be the only time over the next three years that I would experience a supernatural peace in the presence of our Lord.

FIVE

A Three Year Journey

So began our three year journey of faith with our
Lord. It proved to be a journey consisting of emotional highs
and lows. Just when we thought we were close to finding the
truth about the man Jesus, we would come to a new obstacle
in our path. You, Peter, seemed to reach great heights of
understanding but they seemed to be soon followed by some
of the lowest depths of questioning. You have never gone
into anything slowly or half halfheartedly. Sometimes I'm
sure you have simply acted on impulse without thinking at
all. I remember the time that Jesus asked who people thought
he was. All the disciples gave what they had heard – John the
Baptist, or one of the prophets, or Elijah. When the Lord
then asked who we thought he was you quickly answered that
he was the Messiah. He commended you for that declaration
and said that the Holy Spirit had revealed this to you. You
couldn't hide your pride at the time but it wasn't long before
you had to swallow that pride. When you rebuked the Master
for saying that he would be rejected and killed only to rise
again, Jesus turned to you and said, "Get behind me Satan.
You don't understand the things of God but only human

things." You went from receiving high praise to being firmly rebuked and consequently humbled.

And then there was the time that Jesus took you along with James and John up the mountain. I wish that I could have been there but I had to wait till much later to hear the story from you and the other disciples about what happened while you were on that mount. Jesus had changed right before you with his garments glowing the whitest of white. And then Elijah and Moses had appeared and begun talking with our Lord. Then, as you admitted later, you quickly interrupted their conversation by saying with pride how good it was for you to be there and you then suggested that they make three shelters, one for Elijah, one for Moses and one for Jesus as if all three were equal. You couldn't be faulted since at that time none of us fully comprehended who Jesus truly was. But again you were humbled when a cloud covered the mountain and a voice said, "This is my beloved Son: listen to Him." And then Elijah and Moses disappeared. Coming down the mountain Jesus told you not to tell anyone what had happened. I doubt if any of you would have said anything anyway since you really didn't know what had happened. You probably questioned whether the experience was real or whether it was just a vision?

Oh the questions that ran through our minds during those three years. Sometimes even now I wonder if all those things we experienced really did happen, but deep down I know they did. I do hope that Mark will soon write down all the things he experienced over the years along with what you have told him about our own experiences so that others can know just what we did experience and come to believe in Jesus for themselves. Such an account would also help to strengthen those believers that are going through this present persecution brought on by the Antichrist emperor, Nero, which is causing some to question their beliefs. Sadly some have even given up their faith.

Even now my mind spins when I think of all that happened during those three years with our Lord. What thoughts went through our minds. There were so many questions as we heard his teaching and saw the miracles that he performed. Oh what miracles! As a fisherman you were so impressed by the times that Jesus calmed the vicious storms on Lake Galilee. I smiled whenever you shared how afraid you, the experienced fisherman, had been in the midst of the storms, especially when Jesus was asleep or not with you. There was that one time when Jesus came walking on the waves to deliver you. All of the disciples thought that he was a ghost. And he then asked you to come to him on the water and you, impetuous Peter, jumped out of the boat and walked on the water until you took your eyes off of our Lord and placed them on the waves around you. It is unimaginable that even after walking on the water that you could doubt our Lord ever again. But the doubts still came.

There were all those healings. The lame began to walk, the deaf to hear, and the blind to see. And there were those outcasts, the lepers that he healed. I still remember the hurt I saw in Jesus's eyes that time he healed ten lepers and only one out of the ten came back to thank him. We knew that God could heal as we had read in our Scriptures of how he had used His prophets as his instruments for healing. When I was a girl I loved to hear the story of the healing of the leper, Naaman. I especially liked the fact that it was a little Jewish slave girl that directed Naaman to the prophet Elisha. I would often fantasize that I was that maid and I felt so proud that I could be used by God to lead someone to Him.

Even when seeing Jesus's healings with our own eyes

we often wondered whether the people had really been healed or not. We also wondered if he truly was a prophet of God or if he was an impostor like the prophets of the other gods. Every nation had their own gods and the Roman Empire had an hierarchy of gods. The Greeks had centers for healing that they dedicated to their healing god Asclepius who was pictured with a staff entwined by a serpent much like the staff in the wilderness related in our own Scriptures. The pagan priests and prophets did possess power. The Torah tells of the magicians in Egypt whose staffs also turned into snakes as Moses's staff had done. Sure his snake ate theirs but the fact remained that the magicians's staffs had been turned into snakes.

We saw the joy and excitement that the healings would produce among the people. I particularly remember the joy in my own heart when our Lord healed my own mother. She had once again fallen sick with a high fever. I was afraid that she was going to die like my father had and that little Martha would never remember her grandmother. So when Jesus left our synagogue that day we begged him to come and see her. When he entered our house and saw mother lying there he simply took her by the hand and rebuked the fever and it immediately disappeared. There was no question that she had been healed as she immediately got up and began serving everyone there with bread and water. Yes we knew first hand the joy that our Lord's ministry produced in the lives of so many in our nation.

We believed that surely the joy produced through Jesus's miracles must indicate that He truly was from God. It was God's heart to bless. Jeremiah our prophet had written that God had plans for us, plans for good and not for evil so that we might have a future and a hope. And there were the times when people had died and there appeared to be no chance of a future or a hope. But when our Lord raised the dead back to life a future and a hope was restored. It was at those times that we would be sure that Jesus was truly the Lord, Messiah, the Son of God. But sad to say the doubts would soon come back again.

There were also the times that Jesus faced the spiritual forces head on. I was present the time that he cast the seven demons out of Mary Magdelene. And you related to me what had happened the day he cast out a legion of demons from two possessed men in Gadara sending them into a herd of pigs that were feeding nearby. I know that I was afraid when any evil spirits manifested themselves but when Jesus was with us that fear always left and it was replaced by an overwhelming peace as those who were possessed were set free.

Jesus also addressed the central issue of sin and I remember the uproar that would arise when he would outright forgive the sins of individuals. It was our Lord's forgiving of sins that produced the most questions and greatest arguments. For who else can forgive sin but God?

As I am being led through the dark, narrow passageways I see many women: servants, prostitutes, wives of soldiers and even prisoners. They remind me of how I began to notice the way Jesus treated women. He was so accepting, kind and gentle. Sure he was rugged having been a carpenter for years. His hands showed that he knew how to use the tools of the trade. He had swung the axe and adze and drawn the saw back and forth as he hewed and formed beams, door posts and frames. He had wielded the mallet and guided the chisel in producing household furniture and farm implements such as carts, ploughs, winnowing forks and yokes. And he wasn't very handsome but still there was a certain attraction about him. Even the children were drawn to him. He showed that he cared about everyone.

Jesus treated women with respect, almost as equals. He never turned anyone away. Maybe that is why so many women followed him. I remember how people, especially the religious hypocrites, would react judgmentally when Jesus associated with women, especially prostitutes. He let women talk with him, draw water for him and even wash his feet. He also forgave them, seemingly looking beyond their outward sins and seeing their inward needs. I vividly remember the time that those religious rulers brought before Jesus the woman who was caught committing adultery. I wondered where the man was who also had been involved in that adulterous situation. Jesus must have thought somewhat the same way since at first he didn't address the woman but addressed the men. He put the onus on to them when he commanded the one who had no sin to cast the first stone. All the men stole away rather sheepishly one at a time oldest to the youngest until not one was left. Then Jesus addressed the woman saying that he didn't condemn her but that she should go and quit sinning. Our Lord had gone beyond the letter of the law to enforce the spirit of the law.

Our Lord always met the needs of others and he never seemed to distinguish between men and women when meeting those needs. He never showed the prejudice that the rest of society held towards women. He never had the attitude of the majority of our religious leaders who were often heard to pray, "Thank God that I was not born a woman."

Whenever anyone met Jesus, man or woman, he or she, would go away changed in some way. Each knew that he or she had been in the presence of someone different, someone special. His words were different, they held authority; his actions were different, they expressed love.

Even when he corrected others you could sense his love for them. Yet with all of this the questions still remained. Was he truly the promised Messiah, deliverer of Israel? Was he the "Son of God"? Was he, as he would from time to time imply, God in a human body? Whatever people thought about Jesus he was becoming more and more popular all the time and this worried both our religious leaders and the Roman political rulers. But it was our religious leaders that would prove to be the ones that would work the hardest to bring about what they thought would be our Lord's final demise, his death.

SIX

Popularity Ebbs – a Change of Direction

As Jesus's closest followers we were caught up in his popularity. We thought that this rise in fame would never end. He was gaining more and more followers every day. Granted not many of them were rich or important. They were mostly the common people; shepherds, fishermen, craftsmen, labourers, and housewives. And yet a few of our religious leaders were becoming more and more inquisitive. I remember how we were both hopeful and suspiciously apprehensive at the same time when the Pharisee, Nicodemus, cautiously came at night to question our Lord. What Jesus preached had intrigued him as it seemed so different from what he had previously been taught; yet to him it seemed to line up better with the Scriptures. What really attracted Nicodemus to Jesus was the fact that he taught with an air of authority. Jesus's words would linger on in his mind and more so in his heart. But Nicodemus had still gone away with some questions having been unanswered. Above all it was hard for him as with others to break away from the religious tradition that had formed over hundreds of years and the culture that had grown up around it. Yet with all the questions, there was still the hope that this Jesus might be the long awaited Messiah that would overthrow the Roman oppressors and establish the Kingdom of David once again.

As this Messianic hope grew the religious leaders became more and more fearful. They were afraid that the Roman leaders would begin to tighten their hold on our nation. The Roman procurator at that time, Pilate, was not known as one to overlook any threat to his rule. He had already put down some uprisings and quite brutally too. He would act even on the slightest hint of an insurrection. There was one time when some Galileans went to Jerusalem to offer sacrifices. Pilate had heard a rumour that suspected these pilgrims of sedition and so he sent his troops right into the temple as they were sacrificing their animals. These troops drew their swords and massacred the men right on the spot. The very blood of the sacrifices mixed in with the blood of our Galilean brothers. In spite of this brutality our religious leaders hypocritically worked openly with the Roman system since it was Rome that was ensuring their positions as long as they kept the peace. And these religious rulers cherished their positions. They loved the prestige and authority over the people that came with those positions, not withstanding the money and other benefits they also received. So with the rise in Jesus's popularity also came a rise in the religious leader's fears and worries. These fears would lead to their scheming and plotting of ways to do away with Jesus and his followers. Each of us took this to heart.

Just as the fears of Jesus disrupting the status quo of the religious leaders grew, the hopes of those looking for Jesus to be a conquering leader to overthrow the Roman rule began to wane. These waning hopes weren't found just among the fanatical zealots or hyper-fanatical assassins, called "sicarii", so named because of the "sicarius" or dagger that each member concealed in their clothing and would use in attacking those who supported Rome, but also among the common Jews who suffered under the heavy Roman rule with its ever increasing taxation.

Jesus's words were not going unnoticed by the people when he had said that his kingdom was not of this world. They wanted his kingdom to be of this world. We, his closest followers, wanted his kingdom to be of this world. We longed for the earthly kingdom of our father David to be re-established or even the kingdom of our more recent ancestors the Maccabees that had overthrown the yoke put upon us by the Greeks. Our present yoke imposed on us by the Romans was even heavier than that put on us by the Greeks. When the two yokes were compared we used to talk of Greece's being made of bronze while Rome's was made of iron.

Jesus was still performing miracles which showed that he still had his power but his teaching seemed to change. It was more and more about a heavenly kingdom. He would tell parable after parable describing "The kingdom of heaven". We had hoped that those blessings Jesus had given on the Mount of Olives would become the constitution for his reign in an earthly kingdom not some heavenly one. But Jesus kept referring more and more to the spiritual kingdom and to himself as being a spiritual ruler not an earthly one. In fact he kept referring to himself as "spiritual things" like heavenly bread and living water. He also talked about existing before our father, Abraham. Many of his followers began to wonder if he was being overwhelmed by his own popularity. Was He becoming deluded and imagining himself to be something more than human, even more than Messiah? Was he becoming a madman? Even we, his closest followers, sometimes had our doubts. I know that I did. But you could not blame us for doubting. Hadn't that great "prophet" and cousin of Jesus, John the Baptist, doubted when imprisoned by that maniac, Herod Antipas? Little did we know that even then there was one of our own number considering a plan to provoke our Lord into declaring himself king, the earthly Messiah.

Then Jesus began talking about leaving. He talked about going to a place where we could not follow. Some wondered if he meant that He was going back into the wilderness or even to another country. Could he be wanting to go to the kingdom that those three magi had come from shortly after his birth? The questions kept coming. We had been with him for almost three years and he had taught us much but still we didn't fully understand. He told us about another helper that would come in his place. Maybe he would explain everything more fully later. Was Jesus going away to recruit foreign mercenaries to fight for him when he did return? He had told us that he would come back for us after he had left.

But then Jesus began talking about dying. Not accidentally but that others were going to take his life from him. We didn't like such talk. You, Peter, protested and we thought that Jesus had called you Satan as he told you to get away from him. We later realized he was not calling you Satan but was identifying Satan as the source of the idea that our Lord should not die for us. But we didn't understand that at the time and this created more doubts. Over time he would try to console us by telling us that he would not remain dead but would rise again. More questions; more doubts. Surely he had shown great power with his miracles but now he was showing what we thought to be great weakness. You vowed to fight for him and the other disciples said that they would do the same.

But it wasn't just those closest to Jesus that had their

doubts. Others were becoming impatient and drawing further and further away from him at this time. Many left following him and went back to their old ways. I remember how one day when Jesus deeply felt this rejection and asked us, his closest friends, if we wanted to leave also. I am sure that he would have let us go if we had wanted to. He never kept anyone by force or manipulation. Once again it was you who spoke out on behalf of the whole group, questioning where else we could go. You assured him that we all believed that it was only he that had the true teaching and that he was the "Messiah, the Son of the only true and living God." But Jesus told us that one of those He had chosen, one of His twelve closest friends, was a devil and would betray him. More questions; more doubts.

One thing that heightened these doubts and questions was the fact that Jesus had promised us the same power that he had. He said that we could do the same miracles that he was doing and even greater ones. He talked about throwing whole mountains into the sea by just believing. But we didn't see much of that power in our lives. We feared the religious rulers and the Roman leaders. We feared the crowds and the raging sea. When Jesus wasn't with us we failed to do any miracles. I remember the time that a man brought his son to us. You along with James and John were up the mountain with our Lord at the time. The young man was demon possessed and had often cried out and thrown himself onto the ground, or into a fire or a pool of water, foaming at the mouth and grinding his teeth. I felt fear, discouragement and even despair when we couldn't see him delivered. Then Jesus came and berated us for our lack of faith and cast out the demon, setting the young man free. Our first response was another question, "Why couldn't we have done that?

Little did we realize that as we began questioning more and more and our doubts grew, that Jesus was preparing himself to face his own death and also preparing us for what would prove to be the darkest days of our lives.

SEVEN

Jesus's Final Week

That last week of our Lord's earthly ministry remains vivid in my mind as it must in yours. It began on such a triumphant note. Jesus had set the preparation for the Passover Seder into motion. Two of the disciples were sent to Bethany to get a donkey and its colt. We didn't know if it had been prearranged or not, but when asked what they were doing the disciples answered as Jesus had told them by saying that the Lord needed them and they were allowed to take the animals. So our Lord rode into Jerusalem on the back of the colt as its mother followed directly behind. At that time we didn't recognize this as the fulfillment of the words of Zechariah describing the entrance of the Messiah-King into the Holy City. We wondered why our Lord would choose such a lowly means of transport into Jerusalem. Why didn't he ride a horse or just walk into the city as he had done so many times before?

We were not surprised at the crowd that came out to meet us and how it grew as we descended the Mount of Olives. The people had heard of the recent raising of Lazarus from the dead by Jesus so they began praising God for it and

for all the other miracles that they had seen him perform.
They shouted "Hosanna! Hosanna!", "Our God saves! Our
God saves!" , over and over again. I didn't know if it was out
of jealousy or fear that the Pharisees tried to quiet the crowd
and even tried to get Jesus to rebuke his followers for
shouting out. But Jesus simply told them that if the people
didn't cry out then the rocks would. And you know, Peter,
how our land is so full of rocks. We wondered if Jesus was
about to declare that he was the Messiah and rightful King
right then and there. But instead Jesus stopped and looked
intently on Jerusalem and began to weep. We realized that
these were not tears of joy as he began to talk about the days
when the city would be besieged and laid waste.

That entry was truly a triumph. Many years later we
would be reminded of that day as we would see a triumph in
that other regal city, Rome. But what a contrast between
those two triumphs. In Rome the Emperor rode in on his
mighty steed full of pride and splendour. Jesus rode in on a
lowly donkey clothed in meekness and humility. The
Emperor displayed his plunder of coins, gold, silver and
precious stones, followed by rows and rows of men, women
and children taken as slaves. Most of these were ordinary
people just like ourselves who had done nothing wrong.
They were those who had been working and raising families
looking for some enjoyment out of life but now they were in
chains destined to remain in bondage for the rest of their
lives. But in Jesus's triumphant entry he was followed by
men, women and children not being forced in chains by
soldiers but happily and willingly praising him. Many of
them had been healed or delivered from demon bondage by
our Lord. Also many had been freed from the guilt of their
sins. They were still working and raising families but they
had found freedom and the enjoyment of life that they had

been looking for by following Jesus. So they were singing, shouting and dancing of their own free choice. To them our Lord was not a conqueror but an emancipator, a saviour.

Just as the Roman triumph ended by worshiping at the temple of the Emperor's favourite God, usually Jupiter, Jesus' triumph ended in the temple of His God and father. He simply entered the temple and looked around, began to heal the sick and then returned to Bethany.

Returning to Jerusalem the next day our Lord saw a fig tree with leaves but no fruit and he cursed it. When we saw the tree the following day it was dead. Why had Jesus done this? It wasn't the season for fruit but since the fruit on the fig tree comes shortly after the leaves appear this tree should have been bearing fruit despite the season. Our Lord never liked it when people professed to be something that they weren't. He hated hypocrisy. Jesus then told us that we could have the faith to do similar miracles and even more if we simply asked in prayer. But He added that we had to forgive those that we held bitterness towards. Could doing miracles be tied to whether one forgave others or not?

Jesus entered the temple once again and this time he cleared it as he had done at the beginning of his ministry. We wondered if this time he would declare himself Messiah-King. But all he did was begin teaching the people which angered the religious leaders to the point that they intensified their search for ways to destroy him. He taught much those last few days mostly in parables and we had some difficulty understanding the full message that he was trying to give in some of them. Most of them seemed to talk about people rejecting true authority and about the new kingdom that was coming, the spiritual kingdom of heaven. He talked about people trying false ways to enter that kingdom and about false authority and overburdening people with many laws while not keeping them oneself. Everyone knew that he was speaking about our own religious leaders. He warned about the danger of following these false leaders and what the resulting judgment would be for doing so. He spoke of his upcoming death and the importance of believing in him no matter what happened. He talked about using the gifts that we had been given by God and how when he returned he would judge as to how those gifts had been used.

So much teaching in so few days made our heads spin. All this talk of a new kingdom but no declaration of himself as the long awaited earthly Messiah-King. Oh how we wanted him to make that declaration. I believe that we were all ready to fight for him. I know that you and those two Judases, especially the one that we named "Zealotes", the zealot who had even been associated with the sicarii, were ready. We had often thought and secretly hoped that the reason Jesus had chosen Zealotes as one of his disciples was to help lead in a rebellion against the Roman occupation. But Jesus still spoke about a future, heavenly kingdom along with talk about love and forgiveness.

All this time the religious leaders, Pharisees and Sadducees, kept trying to trick Jesus into doing or saying something that would be grounds for his arrest. They were slow to arrest him without proof of some criminal action because the people had shown great support for him. He was far more popular than the religious leaders since they had taxed the people over and over and had fixed harsh religious laws upon them. But Jesus had supplied the people's needs by healing them and by giving them food. He had forgiven them their sins and provided them with a hope. While the religious leaders hated Jesus and wanted to get rid of him they still feared the people. So they tried all they could to discredit Jesus and get the people to turn on him. If that scheme failed they thought that possibly there was a way to get the Roman government to deal with Jesus. Neither Herod Antipas, tetrarch over Galilee, or Pontius Pilate, procurator over Judea, had any love for Jesus. Maybe one or both of them could help the religious leaders out. They suggested that Pilate could be convinced that Jesus was a threat for rebellion against Rome and that Herod could be persuaded to view Jesus as a rival for his throne, King of the Jews. Surely this could be done. They just had to be patient but ever ready to act if the opportunity should arise.

EIGHT

Our Final Seder with Jesus

As the Passover week drew to a close Jesus had us make final preparation for the Seder, the Passover meal. Little did we know how different this Seder would be from all the other Seders that we had celebrated in the past. In fact it would prove to be the last true Seder before the new sacrament which we called "The Lord's Supper" would take its place for all who believed in him. The Seder remembers the deliverance of the Israelites from bondage in Egypt while the Lord's Supper remembers all believers' deliverance from the bondage of sin.

So Jesus sent you, Peter, along with John to prepare for the meal. I remember how you thought someone else should have been chosen to do this since both you and John were in the inner circle along with James. You could perhaps see John being selected because he was the youngest of the disciples but you were one of the senior members and thought that preparing for the Seder was below your position. You still hadn't grasped Jesus's teaching of the first being last and the last first. Again Jesus had given some strange instructions. You were to find a man carrying a jug of water and to follow him. Fetching water wasn't a job for a man, it was considered to be woman's work. Jesus always seemed to surprise us.

So you found the man as Jesus had said you would and you followed him. He then showed you the room that we were going to use for the Seder. It was an upper room built like the little guest rooms on the roofs of our homes but this room was much larger. You and John did a great job of getting things ready. The low lying tables were set up and the pottery provided. You then arranged for the women to prepare the meal. And what a meal it was. Everything needed to celebrate that which symbolized our deliverance from Egypt so long ago was there. There was the shank bone of lamb, reminding us of the sacrifice for sin; the wine as a symbol of the blood of that Passover lamb; sprigs of parsley illustrating the hyssop used to put the blood on the door posts; salt water describing the tears shed while in slavery; horseradish symbolic of the bitterness of that slavery; Charoseth, that mixture of apples, nuts and raisins representing the mortar used to make the bricks. Oh yes, I must not forget the Matzah, the unleavened bread. This type of bread represented the speed with which the departure from Egypt was going to take place. There would be no time to wait for the bread dough to rise. Little did we realize how quickly things would transpire for us once this Seder meal ended or how dramatic and life changing the events that would follow would be.

So you, along with our Lord and the other disciples, retired to the upper room while the women and the rest of Jesus' followers remained in the room below. We thought that this was a little strange as in the past all things done by Jesus, including the Seder meal, were open to all. But this would prove to be a special night with special needs to be taken care of. I remember how you told me that you were disgruntled from the very first, when Jesus, as host seated the disciples and placed you at the far end of the table away from himself, in the place normally reserved for those who would serve. All the disciples were surprised to see Judas Iscariot being placed at Jesus left, the seat reserved for the intimate friend. You all thought that it would be John who would sit there as you all knew that he was the one that Jesus truly loved. But John was seated on the right of Jesus in the spot usually reserved for the honoured guest. Why was Judas seated in the place of the intimate friend? Judas had never been thought of as being intimate with our Lord or with anyone else for that matter. Looking back we thought that Judas was placed there so that Jesus could reveal to him the fact that he knew of his upcoming betrayal by him without the other disciples hearing. Perhaps it was to keep Judas far away from you since if you were to know of his impending betrayal of our Lord you may have done him some harm. Or Jesus may had seated Judas in that spot to let him know that in spite of what he was about to do that he still loved him.

When you were all seated Jesus began to teach you. These lessons were to be his last and most important ones. They were about being servants and of loving one another. He spoke of his death and sending another and then coming back again. You told me that you were sure that he was going away to raise an army and then come back to free Israel from the Romans since he had also talked about his followers going out like he had sent them once before but this time they would take money and swords with them. But you wondered about him saying that he was going to die. How could he come back and deliver his people if he were dead? Would he fake his death and leave Judea? Again more questions arose.

Jesus then gave you all an example of how you should

show your love and servant-hood as he washed each of the disciples' feet. Not understanding what he was trying to teach, you resisted saying that you would never let him wash your feet. But when Jesus said that if you didn't let him wash your feet you couldn't have any part with him, you fervently asked him not only to wash your feet but your hands and head as well. You still hadn't fully grasped the spiritual meaning of servant-hood or of the washing away of sins. Oh my precious Peter, you have come so far since then.

When Jesus handed out the bread he called it his body and told you to eat it. He called the wine his blood and commanded you to drink it. What did that all mean? He said that we would do this over and over in the future until he returned. This again spoke about his going and returning. But before you could ask about this Jesus talked about someone betraying him and then gave Judas a piece of bread that he had dipped in the common plate. Judas then immediately ran out. Little did you think at that time that he was running out to meet with Caiaphas the high priest to complete his deal to betray Jesus for thirty silver coins. You knew that Judas loved money but you didn't think that he loved it to such an extent that he would sell Jesus to those religious hypocrites who wanted to do away with him. Our brother Paul would later fittingly write to a young pastor, Timothy, warning him that the love of money is a root of all kinds of evil. How incensed you were the time Simon, who had been a sorcerer, offered you money to gain the ability to lay his hands on people for them to receive the Holy Spirit. I remember your pointed language as you told him that he had no part in that ministry because he thought that money could be used to buy spiritual power. You told him that you saw that his heart wasn't right with God and that you perceived that he was full of bitterness and in bondage to sin. You felt that he had wanted to use the things of God to profit monetarily. You urged him to repent in the hope that God might forgive him for thinking that way.

But I digress. After Judas ran out you made the declaration that you would fight for Jesus even to the point of laying down your life for him. I know how hurt you must have felt when Jesus responded by saying that you would deny him three times before the rooster would crow twice to welcome the morning. I can picture you, brash, zealous Peter, hotly vowing that Jesus was wrong and that in no way would you, or could you, deny him. And then Jesus prayed for you and all of the disciples for strength for the days to come. How little did all of us realize how much strength we would all need.

We, who had been waiting downstairs, met Jesus and you and the other disciples as you were about to leave. Jesus told us all to go home and to wait for his disciples to return because you were going once more to the Mount of Olives. Why did he say for us to wait for his disciples to return and not for him to return? And why were you going to the Mount of Olives at that hour of day anyway? We didn't get time to ask these questions as Jesus began to sing a hymn and we all joined in. Even before we had finished singing, you, Peter, along with our Lord and the other disciples had disappeared from our sight into the darkness of the night.

NINE

Betrayal and Denial

I remember, Peter, how you told me that the night of our Lord's last Seder seemed so much darker than any other as you and the other disciples followed him the short distance to the foot of the Mount of Olives. You left the city through the Gate of the Essenes as it was the only gate open at that time of night. This gate was also known as the "needle's eye" because of its small size. I still remember when Jesus used it to describe how hard it was for a rich man to enter the kingdom of God, just like how hard it was for a camel to enter through this gate. The load that the camel was carrying would have to be taken off first, just as one must leave his sins before he can enter God's kingdom. As you skirted the Valley of Hinnom or Gehenna, which was where the flames constantly burned in order to dispose of the refuse from the city, you looked up to see the lavish residence of Caiaphas the high priest. You said that at the time you never really thought about Caiaphas but were pondering what Jesus had said about Gehenna being a symbol for the eternal abode of unrighteous sinners.

All the places you passed that night reminded you of your time with Jesus. You remembered the healing of the blind man as you passed the pool of Siloam. Viewing the highest point of the temple reminded you of how Jesus told you that Satan had suggested to him that he should throw himself from that "pinnacle" in order to prove that he was the Messiah. Hadn't we also wanted Jesus to do some great act to prove that he was Messiah?

You could barely make out the outline of the Temple as you descended into the Kidron Valley skirting tombs and gardens as you went. I wonder if these tombs brought thoughts to Jesus of his own soon approaching death. You told me how he tried to encourage you all even as he spoke of upcoming tribulation.

And so you entered the Garden of Gethsemane, the garden of the "oil press". You and the other disciples knew this place well as you and Jesus had been there often before. We all had. The Mount of Olives was where kings and priests of old had been anointed for their positions. The oil used for that anointing was produced from the trees growing on the mount and had been pressed right there in that garden. Oil from the garden's press would also be used to kindle the flame in the Menorah that burned in the Temple.

As you entered the Garden, Jesus had you all stop and then he took that inner circle of James and John and yourself further in to the very middle of the garden being separated from the rest of the disciples. There Jesus asked you to watch and pray and knowing that you were wondering what to watch and pray for he added that it was so that you wouldn't fall into temptation. And you told me that you then wondered what that temptation would be and from where it might come. Always so many questions.

Then Jesus went a short distance further and began to

pray. And while you and the others fell asleep he wept in agony asking if what was about to happen to him could be averted. But when he realized it couldn't he prayed more earnestly until his sweat was mixed with blood and fell to the ground. You told me how our Lord later came and found you asleep and wondered why you couldn't watch with him for only an hour and it was then that you woke and noticed the blood mixed in with his sweat. He came back a second time and again found you asleep and then a third time. This last time he said that you had slept long enough and told you to get up as the betrayer was on his way. And while he was still speaking one of our own, Judas, came with that crowd of temple guards to arrest our Lord. I still cannot understand how he could have betrayed our Lord. Did he love money that much or did he really think that Jesus would destroy them all and set up his kingdom right then and there?

The way that Judas gave the guards a sign as to which of you was Jesus must have broken his heart. Judas showed those angry, hostile men who our Lord was with a kiss, the symbol of brotherly love. And when our Lord told them that he was Jesus the mob drew back with some of the group even falling on the ground. Oh what power there is in his name! And then you, impetuous Peter, seizing the opportunity swung out with your sword and cut off the ear of Malchus, the high priest's servant. Jesus then gently rebuked you and simply touched the man and his ear was completely healed. He reminded you that he had all the power of heaven, including the mighty host of angels, if he wanted to destroy this crowd but that if he destroyed them it would not allow him to finish the work that his Father had given him to do. Again more questions arose. Why heal one who had come to destroy him? Why not fight to protect one's life? What was that work that was so important to finish? Was it so important that Jesus must risk his life and those of his closest friends in order to complete it? We had all forgotten or not fully grasped so much of our Master's teachings.

So our Lord let the angry mob take him only after he asked that his disciples be allowed to leave. And leave you did. You all literally ran for your lives leaving Jesus all alone with his enemies. They then bound him and took him to Annas, father in law of Caiaphas, the high priest. Annas just sent him on to the lavish home of Caiaphas for his son-in-law to deal with him. To your credit and to that of John who went with you, you followed the procession to that home. John was able to enter the courtyard because those in the high priest's household knew him but since they didn't know you, you had to wait at the gate. Shortly John returned having obtained permission to bring you in also. You entered and thus began that period of time during which you would deny our Lord three times just as he had predicted.

I remember how you relayed the story to me in tears. You truly believed in your heart that you would never be able to deny Jesus once, let alone three times. But it only points out how weak we really are even when we feel we are strong. As our brother Paul wrote that there is no sufficiency in ourselves in which we can trust. Hadn't Jesus just shortly before commented that the spirit was willing but the flesh was weak? First you were confronted by a young girl, servant to Caiaphas, as to you knowing Jesus and you denied the fact. And a rooster crowed. Later you denied being one of Jesus' followers. Then finally when they persisted and said you must be one of Jesus's followers because of your rude, Galilean accent and a relative of Malchus whose ear you had cut off said that he had seen you in the garden, you began to curse and adamantly vow that you did not know our Lord. Immediately while you were still speaking, the rooster crowed a second time. And then you saw Jesus looking at you from the porch of the house. What a look that must have been, a look of sadness, not so much for himself but for you. He must have known how you would have felt. But you rushed out and thought about what Jesus had prophesied in the upper room and about what you had just done and you wept with your whole being, from the very innermost depths of your soul.

While this happened outside, Jesus was being tried inside Caiaphas's house by the religious council. The religious rulers had paid witnesses to perjure themselves. This was evident when their testimonies didn't agree. But the leaders persevered and asked Jesus if he were the Christ, the Son of the blessed God. He said nothing and when they continued to press him he finally replied that that is what they had said about him. At this the high priest accused Jesus of blasphemy and sentenced him to death.

And so Jesus was all alone as they took him from Caiaphas's courtyard to the judgment hall of the Roman procurator, Pontius Pilate. Pilate was irritated with having to deal with this case; he had other more important things to deal with, like the raising of taxes for Emperor Tiberius. So when he ascertained that Jesus was a Galilean he seized the opportunity to send him to Herod Antipas who was Tetrarch, or Roman client king, of that province and who just happened to be in Jerusalem at the time. Though he was not a religious person, Herod wanted to placate the people by attending the Passover. He was glad to see Jesus as he had heard about the miracles he had done and was hoping to see one for himself. Jesus had never been impressed with Herod having called him "that old fox", and strangely the word he used for fox literally meant "vixen". When Jesus refused to do anything, not even to utter a word, Herod turned him over to his own armed men to be mocked having him dressed in a royal robe. He then sent him back to Pilate. It is rumoured that Herod and Pilate became friends that day, probably because they had had a common problem set before them – what to do with the man Jesus.

Pilate now wanted to rid himself of this problem as quickly as possible. He hadn't found any reason to condemn Jesus to death just as Herod hadn't found one. So he offered the people a choice of whom he would release to the people at the Passover feast as required by law. The choice he gave them was between Jesus, the miracle worker, or Barabbas, a condemned thief and murderer. Surely the crowd would choose Jesus. But no one can predict how a crowd will react when egged on by a radical few. The religious leaders began to call for the release of Barabbas and the crowd followed suit. Thus the religious leaders got the crowd to ask for the release of a murderer and to demand that Jesus be crucified. So Pilate gave in to the crowd and sentenced our Lord to death on a cross. By doing so he felt that he could appease both the Jews and Rome but that didn't happen. Some three years later Pilate's army killed thousands of Samaritan pilgrims which caused such an outcry in our land that he was recalled to Rome. It wasn't too long after that that we heard he had committed suicide during the rule of the madman, Caligula. We can thank our Lord for the report that Pilate's wife, Proculla, became a believer. It shows that God is not willing that any should perish. Praise his name! Having condemned our Lord to death, the cruel death by crucifixion, Pilate washed his hands as prescribed in our own book of Deuteronomy and declared that he was innocent of this just man's blood, to which the crowd quickly shouted out, "His blood be upon us and our children." And Israel and her people have suffered for this until this very day.

We later heard that it was about this time that Judas, the one who had betrayed our Lord, went back to the chief priests and elders. He had been convicted of his sin and wanted to return the blood money thinking that that would give him some peace of mind. But when the religious leaders wouldn't take the money he threw it down and ran out to hang himself. I am thankful that our Lord is the final judge, full of mercy and love.

So Pilate sent Jesus to be scourged with that dreaded Roman whip with its bits of bone, pottery and lead. These bits would dig into the flesh and tear it away. I remember you saying that when you had a short glimpse of our Lord on the road to the cross you could see some of his ribs showing through. Again your heart cried out within you. Those beating Jesus mocked him, crowned him with a wreath of thorns having long sharp spikes and dressed him again in a purple robe, whose colour indicated royalty. They slapped him over and over crying out "Hail, King of the Jews!" When they tired of their malicious sport they sent Jesus back to Pilate who, thinking that the scourging would be enough to appease the crowd and satisfy the Jewish religious leaders, attempted again to get him released but the crowd cried out louder and louder, "Crucify him! Crucify Him!" Once more Pilate tried to get Jesus set free by saying that he didn't want to crucify their king. All were amazed at the chief priests when they shouted out that they had no king but Caesar. How could they say such a thing? How could they place a pagan Roman in a position of honour above a righteous Jew? Above God himself? Were they really that worried about the possibility of losing their own positions?

TEN

Crucifixion of Jesus and of Our Hopes

With the sham of what the authorities called a trial being over Jesus was led out to Golgatha, the place of the skull, to be crucified. He was forced to carry the heavy crossbeam for his cross but soon stumbled and couldn't carry it any longer due to his whipping and great loss of blood. At this point the soldiers forced Simon, that Hellenistic Jew from Cyrene in northern Africa, to carry it the rest of the way. When Jesus saw people weeping for him along the route, he told them not to weep for him but for themselves. He knew of the troubles that would soon befall them and our holy city Jerusalem. Jesus seldom thought of himself. Even on the cross he refused the gall and myrrh they offered to ease his pain. He had to accept that pain for us so that we wouldn't have to endure it in the future torment of hell.

So they nailed Jesus to the cross crucifying him along with two other "criminals". The soldiers placed over the cross the sign that Pilate had written in Greek, Latin and Hebrew so that everyone would understand it. It said, "This is Jesus of Nazareth the King of the Jews". This greatly angered the chief priest and he asked Pilate to change the sign to say that this is what Jesus had said about himself but Pilate adamantly refused, standing by what he had written. .

While the crowd jeered, the soldiers distributed Jesus's clothes among themselves. They had to cast lots for Jesus's inner garment since it was woven in a single piece and could not be divided. Many scribes and other members of the Sanhedrin, that religious and political ruling body of seventy-one men, began mocking Jesus. They said that he could save others but not himself. Again we saw the selfishness of our leaders being contrasted with the life long "self-giving" of our Lord. Hadn't Jesus said that he could have called the heavenly hosts for assistance and that no one could have any power over him unless it had been given them from heaven. Later, we would understand that this suffering was the plan that God had drawn up and Jesus had agreed to fulfill so that all mankind could receive forgiveness of sins and be delivered from hell itself. For without the shedding of blood there is no remission of sins. Jesus was the ultimate blood sacrifice. We then remembered what John the Baptist had said when he first saw Jesus, "Behold the lamb of God which takes away the sins of the world"."

We saw the evidence of God's plan even while Jesus was suffering on the cross. John, who had gone to Golgotha along with Mary, Jesus's mother; her sister; Mary the wife of Cleophas and Mary Magdelene, from whom Jesus had cast the demons, related to us how the two thieves crucified along with Jesus had at first reviled him for not saving them. But a short while later one of the thieves realizing that Jesus, unlike them, was innocent had a change of heart and asked our Lord to remember him when he entered into His kingdom. Jesus showed his love, mercy and willingness to forgive by assuring this man that that very day he would be with him in Paradise, the heavenly garden, that signified for Jews the dwelling place of the deceased righteous.

Jesus then made provision for the care of his mother. He told her to look upon John as her son and John to look upon Mary as his own mother. From that time on John took care of Mary and continued to do so in the city of Ephesus where he became overseer of the local church. She remained in Ephesus with John until she died and went to be with our Lord in heaven. I am sure that at that time all those things that she had pondered in her heart throughout her lifetime became perfectly clear to her. We often wondered why one of Jesus's brothers wouldn't have taken care of Mary but Jesus always knew what was best.

Then the sky darkened. And Jesus in his suffering felt the total weight of bearing all the sins of the world all alone. He even questioned why his Father and God had forsaken him. He then cried out that he was thirsty and someone offered him vinegar on a sponge which this time he accepted. He then declared that it was finished, commended his own spirit to his Father and willingly gave it up to Him. At that instant our Lord died.

Immediately, great and mysterious things began to happen. The heavy veil in the temple was torn from top to bottom and there was an earthquake which split great boulders and many graves opened up. All these things caused the presiding Roman centurion to cry out in fear, glorifying God and declaring Jesus to be the Son of God and a righteous man. This centurion, now an old man, is still one of our brothers and resides on land near Ravenna in northern Italy given to him by the Caesar when he had fulfilled his time in the army. Even in death Jesus had the power to change lives. Then John, Mary, Jesus's mother, and the other women left the cross and met up with the group of his followers, mainly made up of women like myself, who had been watching from a distance.

I find it hard to describe the grief that we felt as we wailed and smote our breasts. Why weren't you and the other disciples there with us? Only John was there to help console us. Later you told us of how totally in despair you all were. You were in fear for all our lives and were considering what to do next. Your hopes for Jesus being the Messiah and of setting up his earthly kingdom had been utterly crushed. With all hope gone, a deep depression had set in. I am so glad that our Lord didn't wait long to restore those hopes.

Our grief increased as did our questions and doubts when the soldiers took away the body of our Lord. They hadn't had to break his legs as he was already dead when they came to collect the body. This fact even amazed Pilate. All of those that he had seen crucified before needed days for them to die if the leg bones were not broken. The soldiers would often break the victim's bones so that he would be unable to hold himself up and thus be unable to breathe. This was a way of showing a little mercy but it also was used to speed things up so their bodies could be removed and others could be crucified. One of our group pointed out that the fact that Jesus did not have any of his bones broken fulfilled another prophecy that was found in the Psalms written by our father David. Not one of the bones of the Messiah, like those of the Passover lamb, was to be broken. How could so many prophecies be filled and Jesus not be the Messiah?

There was a righteous man, Joseph, from Arimathaea which is just north-west of Jerusalem, who was a secret follower of Jesus because he feared the opinion of the Jewish leaders. At this time he mustered up the courage to go to Pilate and ask for Jesus's body in order to give it a proper burial in his own recently carved garden tomb. Nicodemus, the Pharisee that had questioned Jesus at night, came along with Joseph bringing an ample amount of burial spices which included aloes for fragrance and myrrh for embalming. Jesus's body was wrapped with the spices in linen cloths and placed in Joseph's tomb and then a great stone was rolled over the entrance.

Shortly thereafter, the chief priests and Pharisees came to Pilate asking that the tomb be tightly sealed and guarded for a period of three days. These paranoid leaders had heard Jesus saying that he would rise again after three days and they feared that we, Christ's disciples, would come and steal the body in order to bring credence to Jesus's words. But they had nothing to fear from us as we were too consumed with our own grief, fears, questions and doubts.

ELEVEN

Resurrection – Hope Renewed

None of us got much sleep the night of our Lord's crucifixion and we all stayed behind closed doors on the Sabbath day of rest. Remember Peter, that it was the women who first dared to venture out the following morning. You men were still all too afraid even to go with us as we went to anoint our Lord. We had used the whole Sabbath to prepare the precious sweet spices combining both the spices used for burial along with those used for anointing priests and kings. I remember how Mary Magdalene voiced the question that we all had, "Who was going to remove the great stone from the entrance to the tomb?" It was Salome who replied that with God all things were possible.

As we approached the tomb with the sun just beginning to rise, to our amazement we saw that the stone had already been rolled away. Later we would find out that an angel had removed the stone and that the guards had all fled in fear. When the guards told the chief priests what had happened they were paid to say that the disciples had come and stolen Jesus's body. This false rumour exists to this day in some Jewish circles. I remember it being raised when we were in Babylon. Little did anyone know how impossible it would have been for the disciples to have stolen the body. This wasn't just because of the guards posted at the tomb but also because of the great fear and depression that had rendered the disciples incapable of doing or even thinking of doing anything other than what would help them avoid being discovered by the authorities.

So we entered the tomb but the body of our Lord was not there. We all wondered who could have broken in and stolen the body. It wasn't the disciples and it certainly wouldn't have been the religious leaders as they didn't want the predictions of a resurrection to appear even in the slightest way to be true. Could it have been the zealots, the sicarii, looking for a way to gather more followers and begin a revolt to overthrow the government? But before we could come up with any other suggestions as to the disappearance of Jesus's body two angels appeared. They were dressed in glorious shining robes and we fell to the ground in fear. They asked why we were looking for one who was alive in the resting place of the dead and then they reminded us of how Jesus had told us that he would come alive again after being in the grave for three days. They then told us to go quickly and get the disciples and you Peter. Yes, they specifically named you. We thought that was odd. Was it indicating that you were still counted as part of the group even though you had denied our Lord three times? Or was it an indication that you were to become the leader of our group? But why would you have to lead the disciples if Jesus really was alive? All these questions and many more revolved in our heads as we ran back to give you the news. Oh the mix of emotions we were experiencing – fear, amazement, and astounding joy. Being careful not to say anything to anyone along the way we truly trembled as we ran back to where you were hiding.

When we related to you what we had experienced, you still being gripped with fears and doubts didn't believe us. We also told you that the angels had said that Jesus would meet us in Galilee. But you, impetuous Peter, along with John, the one who loved Jesus so much, ran to the tomb to see for yourselves. John being younger beat you to the tomb but knelt at the entrance looking in while you ran past him right into the tomb itself. You saw the linen head wrap and body cloths but the body was gone. John then entered and saw for himself and only then you both believed what the women had told you. But you still didn't know what was happening or remember all that Jesus had told you about his rising from the dead. So you ran back to the others.

We thought it strange that the first person that Jesus would appear to after his resurrection was a woman. It was to Mary Magdalene from whom our Lord had cast out seven demons that he first appeared as she was weeping at the tomb. When she first saw him she didn't recognize him, possibly because of her tears or maybe it was because of his changed appearance. She addressed him as the keeper of the garden in which the tomb was located and asked him where they had taken Jesus's body. Oh the joy she must have experience when he called her name and she recognized his voice. Jesus had said that his sheep knew his voice. She addressed him as Rabboni, her master, and when she went to grasp hold of him, he told her not to hang on to him as he had to first go to his Father. He then added that his Father was also our Father, his God and our God. When Mary told us this, again we wondered what it all meant.

We were eager to go to Galilee and see if we would truly find Jesus as he said. But he would meet us briefly in Jerusalem before then. Jesus met Cleopas and Mark on their way to Emmaus as they were discussing what had happened during the Passover. They didn't recognize Jesus as he joined them so he asked them why they were sad and what they were talking about. They told him about the Lord's crucifixion and burial and how the women couldn't find the body that very morning. They said that when the disciples had gone to the tomb they couldn't find Jesus's body either. Then Jesus scolded them for not wanting to believe the prophecies of old. He then explained to them the Scriptures from Moses onward that related to himself and especially to those things that had just happened over Passover week. The two disciples were so full of questions that when they neared Emmaus and Jesus indicated that he was going to continue traveling they implored him to stay overnight with them and he agreed to do so. While they were eating the evening meal, our Lord took the bread and broke it and passed it to them. And immediately they recognized the stranger as Jesus. Was it the breaking of the bread that opened their eyes? And then Jesus instantly vanished. Had they really seen the Lord or had it been a vision? So they got up at once and hurriedly returned to Jerusalem remembering how their hearts had burned within them as Jesus expounded the Scriptures to them just a few hours earlier.

Arriving at Jerusalem late that evening Cleopas and Mark banged on the locked door where the disciples were staying. The disciples were reluctant to open the door as they were still afraid of those Jews that had called for the crucifixion of our Lord. When the disciples finally let the two in they explained that they had met Jesus while traveling to Emmaus but the disciples wouldn't believe them. Then Jesus appeared among them in the room and chastised them for their unbelief. I remember how afraid we were and how we thought we were seeing a ghost. But when our Lord knew what we were thinking he told us to touch him since a ghost didn't have flesh and bone. I remember thinking it strange that he said "flesh and bone" and not "flesh and blood" as most would say. Could it have been that he was emphasizing the fact that he had poured out his blood on the cross for our sins? We were overjoyed but many of us still couldn't believe that it was truly Jesus risen from the grave as a real live person. And so to prove it to us once again, he took a piece of broiled Tilapia and a morsel of honeycomb and ate them. He then went over the prophetic Scriptures but this time he opened up our minds so that we could understand them. What enlightenment I felt and an exhilaration as those Scriptures came alive in me and the others that were present. We now understood what he had meant about rebuilding the temple in three days. He had been talking about his own resurrection after three days in the grave. He commanded us to go to the whole world and let others know and if those who heard our message believed it they too would be saved and be able to perform miracles just as he had done. He said that we would receive the Holy Spirit and that we would be able to remit and retain the sins of others. Once again the doubts and questions came. Surely only God could forgive sins? But could we forgive others the sins done against us, thus releasing them from the punishment for those particular sins?

Do you remember dear Peter how Thomas hadn't been with us that first time that our Lord met with us? Think back as to how he wouldn't believe us when we told him what had happened and how that he had said that he would only believe if he saw the nail prints in Jesus's hands for himself. He added, that he would not just have to see the nail prints but that he would actually have to put his fingers into those prints. He would have to thrust his whole hand into the wound where blood mixed with water had poured forth. This was the wound caused by the spear lunged into Jesus side by the soldier after the crucifixion to ensure that Jesus was truly dead. Blessed Luke would later say that through that blood Jesus had redeemed the church and he acknowledged it as being God's own blood. Because of Thomas's unbelief at that time, he was to be nicknamed "Doubting Thomas". I feel that that was rather unfair. Hadn't we all doubted at one time or another?

Eight days latter we all came together and this time Thomas was with us. Once again our Lord appeared to us. This time we wondered how Jesus had gotten in as the doors were locked. He greeted us with the customary "Shalom", "Peace", and then directly addressed Thomas telling him to look at the scars from the nails that pierced his hands and to place his hand into the scar in his side. He wanted Thomas to quit doubting and believe. This convinced Thomas even without him having to touch Jesus's wounds and he immediately declared Jesus as his Lord and even more, his God. Thus this doubter preceded us all in the recognition of who Jesus really was. He was more than a prophet, the Messiah, or even the Son of God. He was God! Jesus remarked that Thomas believed because he had seen but there would be others who would not see him and would still believe. These ones would be equally blessed. When Jesus left us we departed for Galilee.

TWELVE

Return to Galilee and the Command to Wait

We had had enough of Jerusalem with its harsh political government and hypocritical, ritualistic religious leaders. We felt that we needed to spend some time in that gentler, more serene and much safer part of our country, Galilee, where our Lord had conducted most of his earthly ministry. We felt that we needed to process all that we had recently seen and heard. Besides hadn't Jesus said that He would meet us in Galilee?

Since we needed funds to provide for our needs, you and your brother Andrew, along with James and John, decided to go back to what you knew best, fishing. So you returned to your boats and to your nets. I could see that you enjoyed being back fishing. You were a fisherman at heart. But it wasn't quite the same as before you had met Jesus. Hadn't Jesus told you and the other fishermen disciples that you would be fishers of men? Did you ever sit and ponder what that really meant? I know that I did.

I remember the day that you and a number of the disciples were just sitting around and you abruptly got up and said that you were going fishing. You had tired of going over and over those last few days so you wanted to get away from all the questions and theories being tossed about and wanted to be alone. But the rest of the disciples said that they were going to go with you. And so you fished all night without catching anything. What a mood you must have been in that morning. You never liked it when you didn't at least catch enough fish for a meal. So that dawn when you saw a man standing on the shore asking if you had any food, you wanted to get rid of him and answered with a curt "no". You thought that he would then move on but he told you to cast your nets on the right hand side of the boat and you would get fish. I remember you telling us that you didn't know why but you obeyed and the net was overfilled with fish. That is when John recognized that man as our Lord and you, once again the impetuous one, had to act. This time you jumped into the lake and swam to shore while another boat had to come alongside to help drag the net full of fish, all one hundred and fifty of them, to shore.

On shore you saw that Jesus had already prepared bread and fish over a fire of coals. He then invited you all to come and eat and none of you had to ask who he was as you all recognized him as our Lord. And you all breakfasted on fish and bread. After eating Jesus picked you out and called you by your old name of Simon and asked if you loved him more than these. Not knowing what he meant by "these", whether more than the provisions of bread and fish or more than your trade of fishing with its boats and gear, or more than the other disciples loved him, you simply answered that Jesus must know that you loved him. He told you to feed his lambs. What did Jesus mean? First he had told you that you would catch men and now you were to feed lambs. He asked you a second time and when you answered the same as before he told you to feed his sheep. First lambs, now sheep. What was he meaning? Again Jesus questioned your love. This third questioning hurt deep inside your innermost being. You could only answer that Jesus knew the truth, that He knew that you loved him. You didn't rigidly hold on to your own assertion that you loved Him. Why did our Lord question you three times? Maybe it was because you had denied him three times after you had assured him that you would never deny him even once. Perhaps you were still holding on to your own strength, your own ability to love. Again Jesus told you to feed his sheep. And that is what you have been doing from that point of time to this very moment as you face your imminent death, caring for our Lord's followers which he called his sheep.

When our Lord spoke of your future imprisonment and death he exhorted you to follow him in spite of when or how that would come about. Hearing this you then wanted to know what would happen to John. Were you seeking some condolence if John would suffer some tragic end as well? As some say, 'Misery likes company.' Or didn't you know what else to say? Peter, you always felt that you needed to say something. So Jesus told you that what happened to anyone else didn't matter when it came to what you should do. You were to follow him whether John lived forever with no problems at all. And so our brother John still lives and ministers in Ephesus and here we are in Rome ready to meet our Lord.

A short while later Jesus visited us once again and still some of us doubted. How hurt he must have felt because of our unbelief. But he also knew that not too far in the future the Holy Spirit would come and help us with our doubts and answer our questions. He commanded us to go and teach others what we knew and that he would be with us forever. I remember wondering how we women, both married and single, would fit into this plan. To further help us with some of our doubts he showed himself to some five hundred of his followers at one time. He also showed himself to James and others, teaching them about the kingdom of heaven over a period of forty days.

He then told us to wait in Jerusalem until he sent the one that the Father had promised that he had talked about before. This was the Holy Spirit, the Spirit of God. What was this Holy Spirit like? Was he a man, like Jesus? When would he come and how would we recognize him? Would his coming restore the kingdom of Israel? So many questions and so much we still didn't understand. Jesus said that there would be some things that we wouldn't understand now but that we were to wait until things happened in their own proper time. One thing he did assure us of was that when the Holy Spirit came we would know it and that we would receive supernatural power that would enable us to spread his teaching the world over. And Peter we have seen much of this these last few years with the message reaching even the heart of the Empire, Rome itself, with some believers even residing in the emperor's own household.

So he led us to Bethany and blessed us and then on to that familiar spot, the Mount of Olives. It was there that he went up into heaven, a cloud covering him so that we couldn't see him any more. Then two angels appeared and asked us why we were standing around looking up into the sky. They told us that we would not see our Lord again until he came back in a cloud, the same way that he just had left. The angels disappeared from sight and at that time all we could do was worship our Lord. When we had finished worshiping, we returned to Jerusalem to wait for the Holy Spirit that Jesus had said his Father had promised to send to us.

What were we to do until the promised Holy Spirit came? How long would it take? We decided that we should all stay close together and continue meeting in the temple every day, praising and blessing God. And so we did, unsure of what would happen next.

THIRTEEN

Promise Kept – Power Bestowed

I remember when we were in the upper room, that large guest room on the top of a roof, that you, Peter, along with John had rented in the center of Jerusalem. All the disciples with their wives, the other women and many of the children were going to remain there until the promise from God would come. There were one hundred and twenty of us all together. We were a close-knit group. Why shouldn't we be one? Hadn't many of the group frequently been together as they followed Jesus's ministry over the last three years? And the inner circle of disciples had been constantly with our Lord during that time and knew each other intimately.

When, how and where this promise from God would come we didn't know. We certainly didn't know what or who it would be for certain. We trusted that we would know for sure when the promise arrived. Hadn't Jesus often said that he didn't want us to be ignorant or uncertain of anything? None of us wanted to be away from the room for any length of time in case we were to miss out like Thomas did the first time Jesus had appeared to us. I don't think Thomas left at all during this time except for the times we all went to the temple together. The questions and doubts grew as the days went by.

Peter, I remember how you became increasingly restless. You were never one to sit around and do nothing. So I wasn't surprised when one day when you stood up and said that David's writings prophesied that we should chose one to replace Judas in our inner circle. Was your action prompted by God or was it just your own self wanting to fill in some time by doing something different? Whichever case was true the rest of us accepted your suggestion to select some one from among those who had been a follower from the beginning to fill the empty position. You always had a way about you that caused men to follow you. So the names of two men were presented to chose from, Joseph who most knew as Barsabas, surnamed Justus, because of his honourable and righteous character and Matthias who had been one of the seventy that Jesus had sent out. When we couldn't come to a general consensus as to which one to choose we resigned ourselves to using the age old method of "casting of lots". Hadn't the scriptures themselves said that while men might cast the lot into the lap, it was God who determined the outcome? It is sad to say that this practice is used by some at this time for gambling, but that wasn't our intention. We seriously believed that God would make the right choice through this practice. So the lots, various flat coin-like stones that were easy for us to find, were cast and Matthias was chosen. God had made the choice for us. The vacant position was now filled and once again there were twelve disciples which we felt corresponded to the twelve tribes of Israel.

A week passed and more and more we wondered if the promise would truly come. Had we really seen Jesus?

Was it truly him who told us to wait? What if nothing happened? How long could we stay in the upper room? We would soon need more provisions which would mean that some of the men must go back to Galilee to fish once again. We truly didn't know what to do. We prayed and all that would come to mind was, "Wait". So wait we did.

I, for one, was grateful that we didn't have to wait much longer before God sent his gift. You, Peter, were getting more and more impatient and I might say less easy to live with. You would pace up and down and answer roughly when anyone ventured to speak to you. Everyone tried to avoid you as much as possible, including myself. As I said we were all glad that we didn't have to wait too long. I believe God knew how much we all, and you in particular, could endure.

We were nearing Pentecost, the Harvest Feast or Feast of Weeks. So we were preparing the loaves to offer to God in thanks for the harvest. This ceremony would complete that which was started with the waving of a sheaf at Passover and it would represent the dedication of the harvest to our God who had given it and to whom our land and people were holy. In the midst of this feast when we should be thankful and joyful, we still felt a little sad as we realized that at this time most of our harvest would be taken by the agents of Rome to feed the Empire's soldiers who were occupying our land. But we truly were thankful for the little that we did get to keep.

On the Day of Pentecost itself we were about to present our two loaves to God when suddenly we all heard a tremendous noise like that of a great storm. It seemed to fill every corner of the room. As we looked around to see what was happening we saw what looked like flames of fire resting on each of us. Then we all began to speak in different languages; ones we had never learned. Deep inside of us we knew that we had been filled with the Holy Spirit, and that this was the promise from God, and that it was he that was causing us to speak. This was the first time any of us had seen or experienced any thing like this but we didn't question it at all. We would experience these times of being filled with God's Spirit over and over again in the future and each time there would be the experience of speaking in new languages.

You could imagine the noise in that upper room as everyone was loudly proclaiming the wonderful things that God was doing. We weren't talking to anyone in particular. Maybe we were just expressing our feelings of joy to God himself. Those outside who heard the noise began telling others and soon a great crowd gathered around the house where we were staying. This crowd included Jews from all over the world as many had remained in Jerusalem after the Passover, choosing to celebrate Pentecost in the holy city as well since they had traveled so far to get there. They were amazed as they heard us using the languages of the countries from which they had come. There were Jews from Parthia, Media, Elam, Mesopotamia, Cappadocia, Pontus, Asia, Phrygia, Pamphylia, Libya, Crete, Arabia and even from the capitol of the Empire, Rome. These visitors were even more amazed when they found out that we were Galileans better known for our fishing skills than for any aptitude for linguistics.

The onlookers were filled with doubts and questions. How could this happen? What caused it? Was it some strange dementia brought on by stress, illness or demonic spirits? Some tried to laugh it off by saying that we were all drunk. But we in the upper room knew what had really happened. God had sent his promise to us, the Holy Spirit. Our questions passed away as our understanding was opened.

So our Lord chose to use you, Peter, to explain it all to those assembled in front of the house. And explain it you did in a way that I had never seen you express things before. You had always been so abrupt in the past but this time you took time to carefully clarify in full what was happening. You began by firmly stating that we were not drunk since it was only nine o'clock in the morning and there hadn't been time for us to all get drunk. Then you explained that this had been prophesied by the prophet Joel and you quoted those Scriptures. You then went over the ministry of Jesus and how he had been crucified and had risen again. All this you said had been prophesied by our father David and what they now saw and heard was what God had promised to give to us after his Son, Jesus, who they had crucified, had returned to heaven. When the crowd heard about the crucifixion of Christ they were afraid and asked what they should do.

I will never forget how clearly you spoke as you told them to repent and be baptized in the name of Jesus the Messiah and how their sins would be forgiven and they too would receive God's gift of the Holy Spirit. I had never heard you speak with so much authority before. You then told them that this promised gift wasn't just for them but for their children also, and for their grandchildren. In fact it was for anyone, anywhere, at anytime; for all those that our Lord would call.

And oh how that crowd responded. Some three thousand people believed what you said and were baptized that very day. Was this what Jesus meant when he told you that you would fish for and catch men? I still wonder how the religious leaders felt when they saw us baptizing such a large number of people. We used any water available, the pools throughout the city as well as the religious leaders own mikvahs, those baths used for purification when going up to the temple. I can only imagine that they were angry and somewhat afraid.

What joy those first few days following Pentecost held for us. There were three thousand new followers of our Lord added to our small group of one hundred and twenty on that very first day. Oh what dreams and hopes we had for the future. Those new believers were committed from the very first. They so wanted to learn more. They quickly came to believe all that we taught them and they associated themselves closely with us daily. They met with us for prayers and teaching; they even ate with us. They were fearful and amazed as they saw the disciples performing miracles – people healed and delivered from demons. They were so committed that they began selling the things they owned and freely giving the proceeds to us to be distributed among all so that none would have any needs. I remember thinking that you, Peter, wouldn't have to go back fishing. Would you sell your boats? We still didn't know what lay ahead. We were all so united at that time as we met daily in the temple. We were so happy as we praised God and enjoyed the favour of the general population. And every day new people would become believers and join our group. How long could all this last? Could all of Israel believe and be saved? And would this help to free us from Roman rule?

FOURTEEN

Signs Following – Early Opposition

You remember, Peter, how the favour that we had received from the people at that time wasn't held by the high priests and other religious leaders. I remember when you and John went to the temple that one day when the lame man at the gate asked for alms. You quickly told him that while you didn't have any money you would give him what you did have. And then in Jesus's name you commanded him to get up and walk. Picking him up by the right hand he received his healing and immediately began walking and then leaping while all the time he was praising our Lord.

What a stir that caused. Everyone knew that that man had been lame from birth, some forty years, and they had passed him many times as they went up to the temple. Since you were empowered by the Holy Spirit in the upper room you were a changed man. You knew what the people were wondering and you began to preach, explaining what had happened. You let them know that the cripple wasn't healed through any power that you had but through the power of Jesus, by simply having faith in his name. There must have been some of the religious leaders in the group as you talked about how they had rejected Christ and had him crucified. You told them to repent and that they would be forgiven their sins and be sure that after they died and were buried they too would be resurrected. That's when the priests and captain of the temple guard came. They were greatly upset that you taught about the resurrection of the dead since most of them were Sadducees who didn't believe in a bodily resurrection. They arrested you and kept you in jail overnight.

When we heard what had happened we were afraid. What would they do with you? So we all began to pray for your safe release. We now realized that things were not always going to be easy for us. But we rejoiced as we made our prayers on your behalf because of the news that another two thousand men had believed after hearing your message bringing the total of new believers to about five thousand.

The day after your arrest Annas and Caiaphas and the other religious leaders had you brought before them and they demanded that you tell them by whose authority and in whose name you had been preaching and healing. I remember, Peter, how you told us that you felt the Holy Spirit come on you so that you could answer boldly. You told them that if you were going to be questioned over doing a good deed then you would gladly admit that it had been done by the name of Jesus whom they had crucified. You boldly avowed that any true deliverance whether spiritual or physical could only be accomplished through that name. The boldness that they saw in you made these leaders marvel because you were unlearned, simple fishermen from Galilee, that area despised by so many of our religious leaders. And they made a note that you had been with Jesus.

I remember how before Pentecost we had wondered how we could get along without Jesus but since the Holy Spirit came it felt like our Lord was still with us. Is this what

Jesus had meant when he said that he would always be with us to the very end?

The religious leaders felt that they couldn't do anything to you since so many had seen the healing of the lame man. So they said that they would let you go if you would quit preaching and teaching in Jesus's name. But you let them know that you couldn't help but share what you had seen and heard. You had to listen to God rather than to them.

When they let you go you quickly came to us and told us what had happened. And when we heard the story we all began to praise God and asked him to give us the strength to preach our message even more and to see miracles happen in Jesus's name in spite of the threats of the religious leaders. And once again the Holy Spirit shook the place where we were staying and filled each one of us, enabling us to boldly proclaim the message of our Lord. But from then on we would wonder if or when the religious leaders would try to carry out their threats.

For some time the believers settled down together being one in mind and soul. We truly enjoyed the warm fellowship that we were experiencing. None of us had any needs as many of the believers were still selling their possessions, houses and property and giving the proceeds raised from them to the disciples to distribute to any that had need in our group. I particularly remember Joses Barnabas, a Levite from Cyprus, selling his land and giving the monies to us. But not all were so generous. How can we help but remember the case of Ananias and Sapphira? Ananias lied about how much he had gotten for what he had sold. After you confronted him about his lie, he died right there in front of us. And when three hours later his wife told the same lie, she too dropped dead at your feet. They didn't receive this judgment from God because they had withheld some of the

money since no demands were ever made on any of the
believers as to how much one had to give. They could have
given whatever amount they wanted. They were judged
because they had lied to the Holy Spirit. They had lied to
God himself. This incident produced a holy fear in all of us
and caused us to live more righteously. It surely is a fearful
thing to fall into the hands of an angry God. This incident
truly strengthened our young group. We saw many miracles
performed by the disciples at this time, people healed and
delivered from demons. I remember how we were amazed
when the sick were healed as your shadow passed over them.
We wondered what else we were going to see happen in the
future. More and more believers were being added to the
group, both men and women, but those who were merely
curious were afraid to come too close to us. Our group grew
so much that we now began meeting in Solomon's porch, that
great colonnade on the east side of the Temple.

That is when things began to change for us. The high
priest and the Sadducees were feeling threatened by our
popularity and growth in numbers. So they sent the temple
guard to come and arrest the disciples. Were they ever
surprised when they sent to the prison for you the next
morning. The prison was still safely locked up but all of you
were gone. I wish I had been in the prison when the angel
had released you. I had to smile when the religious leaders
became so angry when they found you preaching in the
temple as the angel had commanded you.

When these leaders once again had you presented
before them they asked why you didn't obey their command
not to preach in Jesus's name. It was you again, Peter, who
answered for all the disciples. You told them that you had to
obey God instead of men. You relayed once again how they
had crucified our Lord but he had risen from the grave,

ascended to heaven and sent the Holy Spirit. I don't think they really understood what you were talking about but they were afraid and sought a way to have you killed. One expert in Jewish law, Gamaliel, told the others not to take you too seriously since other groups had arisen in the past and hadn't lasted. He added that if you were truly being led by God it would be useless to oppose you anyway. He felt that if they simply left you alone you would just disappear. So the council decided that you should be beaten and once again commanded you not to speak in the name of Jesus. So we all rejoiced that we were worthy of suffering for our Lord and kept on teaching daily in the temple and from house to house.

And from that time on we realized the danger that the religious leaders held for us. Since they were Jews like us we really didn't know just how intense the persecution from them would be. We all had expected opposition from the Romans but they didn't bother us at that time.

FIFTEEN

Persecution and Flight

Not only were we facing difficulties from the religious leaders outside of our group, we began facing troubles from within. While God hates division, our enemy, the devil, loves it. Remember how those Hellenistic, Greek speaking believers felt that their widows weren't being cared for as well as the widows of the Aramaic speaking believers were? Jealousy is a dangerous emotion. We were all Jews and all believers so the devil thought that he could use the suspicion of prejudice in this situation to divide us. But we quickly solved that problem by appointing seven deacons to look into these allegations and to take care of all widows equally. The disciples could then fully concern themselves with prayer, preaching and teaching. So one internal attack was solved and more people were believing our message. Even some that were members of the priestly circle believed. But darker days were about to overtake us. We were to soon see the first of our group murdered for his faith in our Lord. Little did we know at that time that it would be, one of those first seven men, full of the Holy Ghost that we had just appointed to be deacons.

Stephen, being full of faith and performing many miracles, was a great witness to our Lord. I remember the day when he was out teaching and a group of "Libertines" or "Freedmen" encountered him. These men had been taken from Judea to be the slaves of Roman generals throughout the Empire. In the lands where they had been taken they held on tenaciously to their Jewish beliefs, even more so than those living in Judea. When they were set free and returned to their homeland they often confronted the local Jews. When these men began debating with Stephen and couldn't win they stirred up the people to take him before the religious leaders.

Standing before the Jewish council and being accused of blasphemy, not against God but against the temple and the law, Stephen was once again filled with the Holy Spirit and his face shone like that of an angel. He then skilfully expounded the Scriptures which his accusers had said he had blasphemed. He accused the leaders of resisting the Holy Spirit that had given them the Scriptures and of having killed the Messiah that those Scriptures had foretold would come. He told them that they were not obeying the very Scriptures that they said they were defending. When the leaders heard this they were infuriated and ground their teeth together in a rage. But Stephen calmly looked heavenward and saw our Lord standing at God's right hand side. When he told them what he saw the crowd covered their ears and dragged him outside and began stoning him to death. Before Stephen died he cried out to the Lord not to charge the sin that they were committing to their spiritual accounts. So in death our dear brother Stephen, our first martyr, gave witness of the love of our Lord by forgiving his executioners.

Do you remember, Peter, how some of our fellow believers told us how Saul, that young Jew from Tarsus, condoned the mob's action by watching over the outer garments of those that threw them off in order to participate in the stoning of Stephen? This young Pharisee had trained under Gamaliel that eminent doctor of the law and was so zealous in his religion and its traditions that he had advanced in leadership far beyond most of those his own age.

So began a great persecution of the church by the Jews in Jerusalem and Saul became its greatest proponent. He was obsessed with arresting all the believers that he could find. He went to our houses and hauled us out and threw us into prison. He jailed both men and women. We wondered when this would stop and many of the believers fled to other parts of our country and even to other nations within the Empire. We were thankful for the roads that the Romans had made that facilitated our flight. It seemed like all the believers had left Jerusalem except the inner core of disciples. We prayed for the persecution to cease but we also prayed that if it didn't that we would have the courage to carry on. Most of us prayed that Saul would be taken out of the way, even to the point of wishing him dead. But God had a better idea and some of the believers began praying a different way. They began praying for his salvation.

With the dispersion of believers we soon found people all over the Empire accepting the message of our Lord. It wasn't just our preaching and teaching that convinced them of the truth but it was also the miracles that accompanied our preaching. People couldn't dispute our message when they saw people healed and delivered from evil spirits. But one of the greatest things that attracted others was the love that they saw that we had for each other.

When Philip, another of those first seven deacons, began preaching and performing miracles in Samaria we remembered our Lord's words about how that when we received power from the Holy Spirit we would become witnesses in Jerusalem, Judea and Samaria. Here was the fulfillment of that prediction and it had happened so soon, just a few years since that first Holy Spirit baptism. But Jesus had also predicted that we would be witnesses to the farthest regions of the earth. We began wondering just how far we would go and when it would take place. Little did you and I think that we would ever go as far north as the province of Asia or as far south as Egypt or all the way to Rome.

So when many believed in Samaria, Philip called for you and John to come and help teach and exhort the new believers. You took me and our daughter along with you and I can still remember the amazement that we all felt when you and John laid your hands on those Samaritans and prayed for them to receive the Holy Spirit and they received that same infilling that we had back in the upper room. We were so full of joy that we preached in all the villages along our route back to Jerusalem.

Soon after, this Philip was called by God to go down to the Gaza desert. There he found an Ethiopian who was under the authority of the Candace, or queen, of that nation and in charge of its treasury. He was reading our Scriptures that were written by Isaiah when Philip met him. Philip joined this man and explained to him these Scriptures and told him about our Lord. This government official believed and was baptized in water. Philip later told us how that within moments after he came up out of the water he found himself in Azotus only a short distance away from the Mediterranean coast. We all marveled as he told us that he believed that he had been supernaturally transported by the Holy Spirit directly to that spot. He then followed the Via Maris, the road following the coast, north all the way to Caesarea.

Again we were filled with joy when we heard that

the man from Ethiopia had returned to his homeland and immediately shared his experience in Gaza and gave the message of our Lord to all that he met. Many believed, even some from within the queen's palace. So in spite of the persecution that we were experiencing our numbers were greatly increasing throughout the Empire.

SIXTEEN

Early Travels, Gentiles and Women

I remember, dear Peter, the year when Tiberius, who was Emperor when our Lord was crucified, died. He was an evil man known for his sexual deviancy and it was rumoured that he was murdered by being smothered with his own bed clothes. But that is not why I remember that year so strongly but that it was the same year that our arch enemy, Saul, became one of us. What a change God can make in a person's life. I am so glad that God's plan for Saul was fulfilled and not ours. Our Lord directly intervened and met him on the road to Damascus in Syria where he was going to search for believers and take them bound back to Jerusalem. We all have heard the story of how Saul was struck to the ground and blinded. But then Ananias one of the believers in Damascus overcame his fear and went to Saul and told him of Christ. When Ananias laid hands on Saul, Saul regained his sight and not only believed in our Lord but was baptized in water and in the Holy Spirit and immediately began preaching the message that he had tried so adamantly to completely destroy. Saul then went into the desert of Arabia and was taught directly by our Lord. Three years later he came to Jerusalem and stayed with us for just over two weeks. I remember how the believers in Jerusalem were afraid of Saul thinking that he was saying that he was a believer just to trick us. I must admit that I was skeptical at first. But Barnabas pleaded Saul's case and won us over and Saul began preaching our message so strongly that the Greek speaking Jews wanted him killed. So we sent Saul first to Caesarea and then on to his home city of Tarsus. At this time we never imagined that our brother Saul would become the apostle to the Gentiles and one day languish in the same Mamertine prison as us awaiting his own death sentence.

Thus with Rome totally consumed with adjusting to a new leader, Caligula, and Saul no longer the persecutor that he once had been, the believers entered a time of peace and it was at this time that you began sharing some of the leadership of the Jerusalem believers with James the brother of our Lord. This gave you more time to travel, preaching to the Jews and encouraging our brethren in other cities throughout our nation.

I remember that first trip throughout the country. I was so happy to be able to travel with you, as this time the women in Jerusalem looked after our daughter for us. What a joy it was to watch as our Lord worked miracles through you. There was that time in Lydda when you told Aeneas who had been laying in bed paralyzed for eight years to get up because Jesus the Messiah had made him completely well. He got up immediately just like the man at the temple gate so many years before. When the people of Lydda saw his healing many believed in our Lord. When the news spread to Joppa the believers there sent for you to come and pray for one of their number who was sick. Tabitha who was well known for her works of charity, making clothes and distributing them to the needy, especially the widows, had recently taken violently ill. I remember how as we entered the city the women came to you weeping as they told you that Tabitha had already died. They took you to where they had lain her in an upper room and showed you some of the clothes that she had made. You had everyone leave the room and then knelt down and fervently prayed. And then you told her to get up. I remember the smile on your face when she opened her eyes, saw you and instantly got up. Did I also detect a look of surprise along with that of joy? Then you presented her to all that were gathered outside the room. There was great joy in Joppa that day and many came to believe in our Lord. There were so many interested in your message that you were compelled to remain there for a number of days. So we stayed with Simon, a tanner, and his family. It was a joy during those days to meet new believers and make many good friends. Over the years we have visited Simon a number of times and have kept in touch through letters. I remember how I ministered to the other women while we were in Joppa, teaching them and praying with them, and how fulfilled and blessed I felt as I did.

At this time you were still just ministering to the Jews. You had always seemed to lean towards the belief that only Jews could be true believers. That way of thinking was being put forth by those Jews within our group that had a Pharisaic background. But God would soon use a Gentile centurion in charge of a cohort of legionnaires to bring you to a right mind on this matter. The group of soldiers stationed in Caesarea Maritima, most of whom were archers, was made up of volunteers recruited in Italy. Their leader, Cornelius, was a Gentile but he was a God-fearing man and was thought highly of by the Jews in the city. He prayed to God daily and showed his devotion to God by meeting the needs of others. This was unusual for a Roman leader but this man was genuinely searching for the truth. Later we heard that an angel appeared to him and told him that God had heard his prayers and that he should send to Joppa for a man named Peter who was staying with Simon the tanner.

Our Lord knew that you weren't ready to accept a Gentile at that time so he had to get your attention in a drastic way. On that morning, just before Cornelius's three messengers arrived, the Holy Spirit came on you and you saw a vision. I remember how I called you for lunch but couldn't get you to come. This was strange since you had just been complaining about how hungry you were. It was like you were in a trance. Later you told me that you had seen a canvas sheet before you that was filled with all kinds of animals which Jews were forbidden to eat. Then you heard a voice telling you to prepare these animals and eat them. You objected strongly and refused to eat saying that you had never eaten anything that the Jews called "unclean". The voice then told you not to call anything that God had cleansed "unclean" . This happened three times and then the canvas with the animals disappeared. And while you were still wondering what the vision meant, the three messengers from Caesarea arrived at Simon's house.

When the three men told you about Cornelius and how he wanted you to come to him, I was amazed that you never hesitated in going with them. I didn't know at that time that the Holy Spirit had told you not to doubt but to go with them because it was God that had really sent the messengers to you by the hand of Cornelius. We were a little sad to be leaving Joppa since we had had happy times there and we wondered what our Lord had in store for us in Caesarea. But I was also excited to be going to Caesarea. This was not so much because of it being a great Hellenistic city with a larger population than that of Jerusalem but as to the fact that it was

there that Philip and his prophetess daughters resided. I
hoped to meet those girls and find out how their ministry
related to the rest of the believers.

Yes, Caesarea was a great metropolis founded by
Herod the Great in only twelve years. He built a great
harbour with its own lighthouse and then he built a theatre,
amphitheatre, and a royal palace. That palace became the
residence and seat of government for those Roman prefects
that ruled our nation and for the so-called Jewish kings who
were mere puppets of Rome. It was here that over the years
Pilate, Felix and Festus resided as did Herod Agrippa and his
son, also named Agrippa. It was an evil city with its bath,
games, and prostitute houses. But worst of all were those
temples dedicated to all the pagan gods, Aphrodite, Serapis,
Mithras and more. Tyche was deemed the protective
goddess of the city. When Herod first founded the city and
named it Caesarea Maritima after the emperor Augustus he
built a temple and dedicated it to the imperial cult, to
Augustus himself and to Rome.

As we entered Caesarea we passed many fountains,
the bath and even latrines all with running water. This was
amazing since the city itself had no fresh water source. Then
we saw the great aqueduct erected out of that beautiful cream
coloured sandstone used so frequently for building
throughout our whole nation. We were told by one of the
messengers that this aqueduct carried water all the way from
a spring on Mount Carmel some ten kilometers away to
provide the water for the entire city. How my imagination
ran away with me as I pictured in my mind our prophet Elijah
getting the water from that very spring to soak the sacrifice
that day so long ago when God answered by burning it up
with fire thus defeating the prophets of Baal. Sadly that false
god is still being worshiped in our day and a depiction of him

is even represented on our own temple Shekel.

So the messengers led us to the headquarters of Rome's Tenth Legion where Cornelius and his family were living. Cornelius met us at the door of his house and fell down at your feet. You quickly told him to stand up because you were just a man like he was. When you entered the house, it was full of Gentiles and you then understood what the vision meant. You realized that God didn't show favouritism towards any one but would accept people from any nation who feared him and did what was right . As you shared with the people the message of our Lord the Holy Spirit fell on them. Again it was just like we had experienced in the upper room but this time it was happening to Gentiles. How could we deny that now God was opening up salvation to other peoples and nations, not just to the Jews? Soon some Jewish believers that had come out of the synagogue in Caesarea showed up and were amazed that Gentiles could receive the Holy Spirit just like Jews, speaking in tongues and glorifying God. We stayed in Caesarea a number of days teaching the believers and sharing our message with the Jews. When we decided to return to Jerusalem I was so pleased when you suggested that we visit our brother Philip before we left. As I said Philip had four unmarried daughters that were renowned for being prophetesses and I was interested in what that meant for women in the church. Hadn't you Peter quoted from Joel's prophecy on that day that the promised Holy Spirit was given of how our sons and our daughters would prophesy in the last days?

When we arrived at Philip's house he welcomed us with open arms and the kiss of fellowship. Since he was a widower it was two of his daughters that extended hospitality to us. They provided water for us to wash our feet and prepared a meal as was the custom. We were surprised to hear that Philip's other two daughters had gone to Antioch to minister in the church there. As you talked with Philip about his evangelistic journeys and of your own experiences, I began questioning the daughters. What did their ministry entail? Was their ministry generally accepted by the believers? They began by explaining how they had received the Holy Spirit at Pentecost and that shortly after that time they had received the gift of prophecy. The Holy Spirit would come upon them in the gathering of believers and they would speak forth the mysteries of God. These mysteries were not predicting the future but were more an expounding of Scripture and a giving of exhortation. When this first took place they really didn't understand what was happening but the messages that they gave were affirmed by Scripture and the elders in the church. The news of their gift spread and other groups of believers asked for them to visit them in hopes that the sisters might have a message from God for them as well. They also traveled with their father from time to time and complimented his evangelistic ministry with their own. They were so happy and felt blessed that they could not only minister to other women but to the whole church in general often setting a foundation for others to build upon in using the gifts that God would give to them. When I asked them about not being married they told me that they were so busy doing the Lord's work at that time that they hadn't thought about it that much and that perhaps they might marry in the future if the Lord led in that direction.

I left Philip's home rejoicing in the fact that God was using women to help build his church not only by supporting their husbands or by dealing with women's issues but by giving direct messages from God to the whole church by the means of the gift that God had given them. When we arrived in Jerusalem, we found out that the news of the salvation of the Gentiles had already reached the brethren there. This had caused a new division to start among the believers in Jerusalem. There were those who were willing to accept Gentiles as believers and part of our group and there were those who were only willing to accept Jews. I was proud of you, Peter, when with authority you simply shared what had happened in Joppa and Caesarea. And when they heard this report coming from you the objections to receiving the Gentiles were silenced and all the believers praised God for the fact that Gentiles could also have eternal life. It was at this time that Zaccheaus, the one who had climbed up into a tree to see Jesus took leadership of the believers in Caesarea.

So the message of our Lord spread as the believers that had fled Jerusalem settled throughout the Empire and we saw more and more Jews and Gentiles believing the message of our Lord.. The new believers needed leaders in their own areas so we began sending out evangelists, pastors and teachers to assist in training and choosing men and women as elders and deacons and deaconesses to lead the groups that were springing up in each city. The area that was growing the quickest at that time was that around Antioch. So you sent Barnabas to get Saul from Tarsus to go there to spend a year training the believers. There were so many believers in that city and so much talk of our Lord as the Messiah or Christ that those in our group there were being called "Christians". This was the first time that that name was used to describe believers in our Lord but that nickname stuck and spread throughout the Empire. We were proud to take that name and we are known as "Christians" to this very day.

SEVENTEEN

Prison and Travel to Asia Minor

So the church grew both in our own nation and throughout the Empire. I remember how things were relatively quiet in Jerusalem and Judea until Satan stirred up Herod Agrippa to persecute this new group known as Christians. The persecution began quickly and dramatically with our close friend James the brother of John being cut down with a sword. Oh how those religious leaders of the Jews were pleased by this. They predicted that this was the beginning of the end for our group. When Agrippa saw how he had gratified the Jewish leaders he decided to kill you, Peter, as well. So he had you arrested and thrown in jail. Agrippa had heard about your previous escape so he held you under the guard of sixteen soldiers to make sure that it wouldn't happen again and that he would be able to execute you soon after Passover was over. To be totally sure that you wouldn't escape they had you double chained between two soldiers with two more guarding the cell door. I was so worried when they took you and I ran to tell the rest of the believers. When they heard that you were imprisoned they gathered together and began earnestly praying for your deliverance.

It wasn't until the night before Agrippa intended to have you killed that our Lord answered our prayers. I don't know how you could sleep that night knowing that the next day you were slated to be killed. The angel that lit up the prison that night had to hit you on your side to wake you. He then told you to get up quickly and immediately your chains fell off. He told you to get dressed and put on your sandals and follow him. You did what you were told but thought that it all was just a dream. You passed two cell blocks on the way to the two heavy iron gates which fronted the street into the city. You were amazed when those gates opened by themselves as you and the angel approached them. The angel went with you for a while and then disappeared at which time you came to your senses realizing that what had just happened wasn't a dream but reality. You now knew that our Lord had sent an angel to deliver you from Herod and the Jews.

You were still mulling all this over when you approached the house of Mary the mother of Mark. It was there that many of us had gathered to pray. I thought that it was quite amusing when the servant girl, Rhoda, came to answer the door when you knocked and upon recognizing your voice became so excited and overjoyed that she ran to tell the rest of us leaving you standing outside. When we heard the news we told her she must be out of her mind or that it was your spirit, or messenger, or guardian angel. But you kept on knocking, harder and louder all the time and when we opened the door and saw you standing there we were all amazed. I remember thinking to myself that our faith really hadn't grown much. Why hadn't we believed that you would be set free? Why had we expected the worst? You told us to calm down and go tell James, the brother of

Jesus, who was now the leader of the believers in Jerusalem, what had happened. He was meeting with another group of believers in the city also offering up prayers for your deliverance. As leader of the faithful he should let all those with him know that their prayers had been answered. Then you and I, with our daughter, left for a safer place. What fear must have rightly filled the prison guards' hearts that next morning when they realized that you were gone. That fear was found to be justified when Agrippa had all the guards killed and being embarrassed by your escape he ran off to his palace in Caesarea.

It was shortly after that incident that delegates from Tyre and Sidon came to Agrippa . He had been upset with the two cities and these delegates were sent to sue for peace with him since the cities were dependent on him for trade. At that time Agrippa called a festival in honour of the Emperor Claudius and dressed himself up in royal robes made entirely of silver cloth. When he got up to speak and the sun's rays shone on him, many flatterers called out that it was the voice of a god, that he was a god. And Agrippa being the man that he was, full of pride, did not stop them from calling out but accepted their praise. It was then that God sent an angel who struck him with an illness, reputed to be worms, producing excruciating pains in his stomach. In five days he was dead. Such is the danger of taking praise for oneself and not giving all the glory to the one true God.

We were so happy when at this time our daughter chose to marry. Her husband was a believer from Antioch and we were sad when she left to live with him there but it did free us up so that we could travel more extensively. And how we did travel! We visited believers where there were churches and preached to the Jews in the synagogues in each area. We traveled north through Syria, Cappadocia, Pontus,

Bithynia, Asia and Galatia. Most of our travel in Judea had been by foot but now with greater distances involved we needed other means of transport. We often borrowed a donkey from a Christian brother and you and I would take turns riding it. We would leave the animal at a brother's house when we had reached our destination so that it could be retrieved later on. I never did get used to riding a donkey and often would allow you to keep riding when it was my turn. I liked it when we were allowed to catch a ride on a cart pulled by oxen or donkeys. The Romans had built stone roads but there would always be dust as travelers passed each other and had to go off the pavement. I would watch in awe and with a little fear as the Roman legions would pass by pushing the other travelers off the road. I loved to see the Imperial post riders on their steeds speeding along with official government documents. There were times we were able to take a raft or ferry and enjoy resting as we floated down the river to the next leg of our journey. It was so peaceful on the water. I always loved the water having been raised in Galilee. After seeing the Black Sea and the Great Sea I wonder how we could have ever called our own small lake in Galilee a sea.

And so we traveled from town to town teaching and preaching, you with the men and I with the women. And the words of Jesus about how we would see miracles came true over and over again. The blind saw, the deaf heard, the lame walked and the demon possessed were set free. What joy followed our ministry as many unbelievers believed receiving salvation and groups of believers were encouraged. Those were happy days as we met new people and stayed in the homes of the believers we met in each region. We would have traveled on right through Greece and then to Rome but we received news from Aquila and Priscilla that Emperor Claudius was angry with the Jews and Christians over the many confrontations that were erupting between them in the capital. In fact it was at this time that the Emperor expelled all Jews from Rome.

Since we had been longing to see our daughter and her husband again we decided to return to the church in Jerusalem and visit with our children on the way. They had had two children of their own, a boy and a girl, which we had never seen so we hurried straight back to Antioch and spent time with the family. I remember you, Peter the big, rough fisherman, gently holding those little ones and singing softly to them in the evening. We were sad to leave and return to Jerusalem but we were thankful to our Lord that we had seen the new additions to our family.

At this time James, now fully in charge of overseeing the church in Jerusalem, called a council of church leaders in the region. It seems that certain believers from Jerusalem had gone to Antioch to convince the church there that to be saved one had to be circumcised like all Jews were. This had caused a division in the church in Antioch so Saul, now know by his Greek name, Paul, and Barnabas were sent to Jerusalem to ask for advice from the disciples and elders there. The Jerusalem church was still considered to be the center of Christianity and all churches throughout the Empire looked to it for leadership. When Paul and Barnabas arrived in Jerusalem they told of all the miracles and conversions that they had seen among the Gentiles during their recent evangelistic trip. They were true apostles or as the Roman officials called them "missionaries" since many of the places they had traveled to had never heard the message of our Lord before. We too related accounts of the works we had seen done by God among the Gentiles in the places that we had visited in recent years. At these reports most of the believers in Jerusalem rejoiced. But there were those who had been converted from among the Pharisees that still felt the need for circumcision of all believers, Jew or Gentile, and that we all must keep the law of Moses. This troubled the Gentile believers so our leaders decided to further look into the issue and try to come to some consensus.

After many days of debate, it was you once again, Peter, who dared to bring the matter to a conclusion. You mentioned how God had used Jewish believers to bring the message to the Gentiles in the first place and that when many of the Gentiles accepted that message, God freely gave them the Holy Spirit just as he had given him to us. How could we burden down these new believers with the laws that our forefathers and ourselves were unable to fully keep? And once again we asked Paul and Barnabas to tell us of what they had seen our Lord doing among the Gentiles. And then James said that this had been prophesied by our own prophets in the Scriptures and gave references. I had never seen those passages in that light before and I was happy to be taught this since I have always loved learning new things. James then concluded our meetings by saying that the Jewish believers should not attempt to make the Gentile believers keep all the laws that were given to the Jews. He did say that they must not partake of anything that had been sacrificed to idols, or eat any meat that had not been properly killed and bled and to flee from fornication. To do those things would be enough. So another attempt at causing division within our group was diverted. Paul and Barnabas along with two members of the believers in Jerusalem, Judas and Silas, took the decision back to Antioch. When the believers there heard the outcome they were filled with joy.

But the issue of division between Jewish and Gentile believers would rise up over and over again. Needless to say, Peter, how disappointed I was in you when Paul had to stand up against you when you later visited Antioch. He did this because you quit eating with the Gentiles when certain Jewish believers sent from Jerusalem by James arrived there. Paul pointed out to you that Jews often lived like Gentiles, not keeping all of the Jewish laws themselves so how could you expect Gentiles to fully live like Jews. I asked myself if we would ever be completely changed and live like our Lord had taught us to by truly loving one another? I guess we won't be perfect and be like our Lord until that day when we shall see him once again.

EIGHTEEN

Asia Minor, Rome and Egypt

After our time in Antioch where we once again enjoyed our children and grandchildren, we decided to travel a second time through Asia Minor. We revisited the places that we had gone during our first trip. It was exciting to see what our Lord had been doing throughout the area. Every church had grown. This time we spent longer in each town than we had before. You so enjoyed teaching the new converts and then going to the closest synagogue to share our message with the Jews. There had been a Jewish presence in the area for a period of some six hundred years since the original Diaspora of our people. Thus there were many synagogues throughout the whole region. Some of the largest and most elaborate with their Greek styled columns and mosaics were to be found in Sardis, Ephesus, Iconium and Bergama. I enjoyed working with the women encouraging them to study the Scriptures and to reach out to other women with our message. This inclusion of women was the one thing about our religion that women liked Women had supported Jesus during his ministry and our brother Paul had preached that in the church there was no distinction between men and women. We did hold to the culture of the day with ultimate authority resting with the men but we also gave women many opportunities to minister. We had set up the position of deaconess to deal with the problems particular to women and their children. These women counseled and taught the other women and assisted with their water baptism. Also women were evangelists and prophetesses in their own right. Sadly during this time we heard that Philip, the disciple not the evangelist, who had moved to Asia along with his two daughters, had been recently martyred. The leaders of a cult in Hieropolis that worshiped the god Mars in the shape of a dragon had crucified him. His grave can still be seen in that city to this day.

We spent a number of years in Asia Minor where we happened to meet up with Mark who had heard that Paul had recently been sent from Caesarea to Rome in chains. Paul had been accused by the Jews of causing division and rebellion against the Emperor and so he was kept under guard in Caesarea by the order of two Roman procurators, Felix and Festus, until he appealed to Rome. Paul could make this appeal because he was a Roman citizen. Mark had heard this news of Paul's departure to Rome in Egypt where he had gone after the Lord's ascension and had founded a church. He told us that a great number of people both Jews and Gentiles had accepted the message of our Lord and that many churches had been established throughout that province. Mark asked if we might be interested in going back to Egypt with him when he returned from visiting Paul since Alexandria where he was now leader had a large Jewish population. You were aware of that fact and had long desired to visit Egypt, the land of Joseph and Moses and where our Lord's earthly parents had taken him for refuge from Herod's anger. Previously you had been hindered from going there but now it seemed as if a door was about to open so that you might fulfill your heart's desire.

You suggested that we might travel with Mark to Rome and visit Paul together. So we traveled to Ephesus where John was the leader of the church that Paul had established there. John had taken Mary, our Lord's mother, with him when he went to Ephesus and cared for her until she passed away in that city. I have often wondered what it was like when Mary and Jesus met once again in that heavenly home. In Ephesus we met with John and a young man named Polycarp who had just recently become a believer. You and I both recognized leadership qualities in him even at that time. From Ephesus we sailed to Corinth and spent some time there preaching and teaching in that great city while we waited for favourable weather for sailing on to Rome. I noticed that many quickly became attached to you, especially those who had been converted from Judaism. Later we heard that divisions had risen up in the church in Corinth over who the believers should follow. One group said that they were followers of Paul, another said that they were followers of Apollos, while still another said that they were followers of you, Peter. Of course there was one group that didn't name any earthly teacher to follow but claimed to be the only true followers of Christ. How sad that made us feel when we heard about those divisions. But the church in Corinth seems to have taken on the character of the city itself with its many divisions in race, culture, status and beliefs. Our Lord hates division and I wonder when it will ever end. Probably not until our enemy, the devil, who loves to cause division is finally dealt with by our Lord.

We soon reached Rome and were able to visit Paul who was not in prison but under house arrest. He was busy writing letters to the churches and preaching the message of our Lord. He had you preach and teach in the church there in Rome. He said that it would be good for the people to hear from someone who could fully present the Jewish roots of our beliefs. Paul had always said that he had been called to the Gentiles, while you Peter had been called to minister to the Jews.

It was at this time that the believers throughout the Empire were experiencing a great amount of persecution. Our brother and fellow disciple, Bartholomew, also known as Nathaniel, who had taken our message as far as India, was hacked to pieces and then beheaded in Armenia. Matthew was run through by a spear in Asiatic Ethiopia, an area of Persia south of the Caspian Sea, where he had ministered. I remember how we wept when we heard that your brother, Andrew, had been crucified by being tied to an X-shaped cross in Macedonia. It is said that it took him two days to die. I was amazed how you could later praise our Lord that your brother was deemed worthy to die such a death. And then there was James, son of Alphaeus, who was a leader of the church in Syria who was thrown from the temple and stoned and then beaten to death with a fuller's club.

With all this happening throughout the Empire it was no wonder that Paul hastily headed towards Spain when he was released from being under house arrest . We too quickly left Rome going with Mark directly to Alexandria. We boarded a ship returning to Egypt after it had unloaded its cargo of grain in Rome. Egypt was where Rome got the majority of its grain for bread. The emperors always said that they needed to give the people cheap bread and free games, those gladiatorial extravaganzas, to keep them contented thus lowering the chances of revolt. Even with favourable winds it took us a week to make the fifteen hundred kilometer voyage to Alexandria. I was thankful for the steady breeze and calm seas. I enjoyed seeing the sails made from flax furl out on the masts and listening to the sound of the wind blowing through the rigging. I also enjoyed the sound of the water hitting the prow of the ship and the smell of the sea air which produced a saltiness on our lips. We watched the many different types of sea birds and the porpoises that followed our ship. Gazing out from the stern we saw the ship's wake which looked like a highway paved with foam. Oh how I love the sea! I wonder if I will miss the sea in heaven but I am sure there will be seas on the new earth. I was not only glad for the good weather on our trip but that we saw no sign of pirates. As a little girl my mother and father had told me stories of pirates that they had heard from travelers. I didn't realize that since the time of Julius Caesar piracy on the Mediterranean had been kept under control. There were only a few brigands left who with government consent provided slaves for the emperors themselves.

Once in Alexandria you, Peter, began seeking out the Jewish population in order to share with them the message of our Lord. Alexandria had been a center of Judaism for years with Jews having come there when Alexander the Great first founded the city. The Jewish population grew and many Jews became citizens and even held public office. Many synagogues sprang up. The Jews in Alexandria were quickly Hellenized and they produced the first copy of our Scriptures in Greek. While becoming Hellenized the Jews in Alexandria still held strongly to the Jewish religion yet used Greek philosophy to defend it. Being highly academic the leaders felt superior to most other Jews throughout the Empire, even to those in Judea. I remember, Peter, how disappointed you were as the Jewish population in Alexandria rejected the message of our Lord.

It was then that one of the brothers mentioned to you

that there was a large group of Jews just a few kilometers south of Alexandria in the fortress of Babylon. So we traveled south and found the Jews there more receptive to our message. I remember how awestruck I was when I first saw the pyramids and that huge, strange sculpture of a lion with a human head. The Egyptians call it the Sphinx or living statue while the Greeks associate it with the mythical winged being that would strangle its victims. It saddened me to think of the great effort that went into making those monuments to mere men and pagan gods. The pharaohs thought that the structures would help them obtain eternal life. I am glad that anyone can receive that life simply by believing in the one true God and his only Son, Jesus our Lord. I pray that our religion will never resort to building such structures. The true God doesn't dwell in temples made with hands and our Lord chastised you for suggesting the building of shelters for Moses and Elijah on the mount of transfiguration. Those colossal monuments that we saw in Egypt reminded me of the story of the bondage that our people suffered under the pharaohs so long ago in the time of Moses. It also reminded me of God's great deliverance from that bondage with the miracles of plagues, crossing of the Red Sea and provision in the wilderness. Jews still celebrate that deliverance at each Passover while we Christians celebrate our release from the bondage of sin through believing in our Lord each Lord's Day.

We remained in the Egyptian fortress of Babylon for some time and many accepted our message. I found it humorous when we learned that some of the brothers in Judea thought that you had gone to the ancient city of Babylon in the east when they heard that you were in Babylon. But that area is now known as part of the Parthian Empire not Babylonia. You had had no desire to go there since the

Jewish population in that area had drastically dwindled to the point that there were very few Jews left. The majority of the Jews of the ancient city of Babylon had moved to the city of Selucia further north and then on to the cities of Neerda and Nisibis. While in Egypt you wrote a letter of encouragement to be read by all the churches throughout Asia and it was also at this time that Mark began writing the story of our Lord taken from your own reminiscences. I do hope that he finishes that story before he too may suffer martyrdom as we are about to face.

    While we were in Babylon Paul was arrested once again and he sent a messenger to find Mark and ask him to come to Rome because he needed him. What a change we had seen in the relationship between Paul and Mark over the years. I still remember when Paul didn't want Mark to travel with Barnabas and him on their second missionary tour since he had abandoned them on their first excursion. Thus the two split, Paul taking Silas with him and Barnabas taking Mark. Many of the believers feared that this split would hinder the spread of our message but in fact it aided our cause with two missionary teams going out instead of one. What the devil sets as evil, God can always turn to good. Thus Peter, I am certain that God will use our deaths for his glory and the furthering of his kingdom. Mark has proven himself over and over since the time he left in the middle of that first missionary trip. He has traveled with Barnabas to Cyprus, founded a church in Egypt, helped Paul in Rome and also been a great help to you Peter. So we didn't find it a surprise when Paul sent for Mark. When Mark said that he was going to fulfill Paul's request and immediately travel to Rome, we decided to go along with him.

NINETEEN

Final Trip to Rome

So here we are in the Mamertine prison in Rome. We were immediately arrested when we landed at the port of Ostia. I still don't know how they knew that we were coming but there were always those in our own group like Judas who would betray us for money or for their own deliverance from persecution. Emperor Nero had blamed the fire in Rome on the believers and immediately stepped up the persecution of the church. This was an attempt to quell the rumours that Nero had set the fire himself in order to have more area to build a new and grander palace and that he had actually played his lyre and sang the classical Greek dirge, "The Sack of Ilium", as the flames consumed the city. Even though he is an evil man and is controlled by the spirit of Antichrist, I do not believe that he lit the fire since he had placed himself in danger by helping to put out the flames. He actually organized a relief effort providing shelter and food for the survivors of the fire. Nero knew that the Christians did not accept the Empire cult, bow down to him or worship any of the Roman gods. He also knew that we would not resist his troops but would rather suffer martyrdom for our Lord. So we became the perfect scapegoats. We had already been accused of incest because of the fact that our husbands and wives call each other brother and sister. In Christ we are all brothers and sisters. More serious was the accusation of us practicing cannibalism. This comes from the fact that we call the emblems of bread and wine that we use at the Lord's Supper the flesh and blood of our Lord.

Many of our brothers and sisters have been imprisoned and killed. Some have been dressed in animal skins and torn apart by dogs in the arena while others have been used as prey for wild beasts or as combatants for the gladiators. I don't think the crowds are very happy when we will not fight but simply gather together and praise our Lord and sing hymns. I wonder how they feel when they hear us pray for the salvation of our persecutors, including for the emperor himself. Nero even coated some of the brothers in tar and lit them on fire in order to illuminate his garden's at night. I have heard that because of the harshness of this persecution there is a growing sympathy for the believers by the general populace with some even helping our brothers and sisters flee the city and providing for them until it is safe to do so. Many of our group have hidden out in the catacombs, those old burial grounds under the city and some unbelievers have even brought food and water to them there.

So we have been in this prison for nine months. Even being kept in separate cells we have been informed of each others circumstances by the brothers and sisters that have visited us and by some of the guards who were sympathetic towards us. We have not been idle during that time as we have both had opportunity to preach our message to the other prisoners and even to those guarding us. We have also been able to strengthen our brethren during this terrible time. I heard that you have even been able to send out another letter by Mark to the believers in Asia Minor. I do hope that Mark will leave Rome before he too is arrested and that he will finish his biography of our Lord based on your own recollections. I know that the Holy Spirit will guide him as what to write and that such a book will help strengthen and comfort all the new believers.

We have had a good life together. It is hard to believe that we have been married for almost fifty years. I have never regretted marrying you, dear Peter. I have been blessed having you as a husband and Petronella as a daughter who has given us two beautiful grandchildren. I have also been so blessed as a woman to have traveled to so many places, seen so many different sights and met so many different people, many of whom have become our brothers and sister and our friends. But the greatest blessing for me has been being a part of our Lord's work. I have been able to learn so much and thus have been able to teach and counsel so many others. I have felt so fulfilled.

Having been imprisoned here in Rome during these last few months you have suffered much torture but have remained strong in your faith. You have maintained your witness for our Lord and have seen forty-nine new converts including two of your jailers, Processus and Maritinianus. But we will soon be set free like a child is freed from the womb when its mother gives it birth. We will be free from this evil and corrupt world and from our own aging physical bodies. We will enter heaven, that beautiful perfect kingdom of God and eventually receive new bodies free from any aches and pains. Best of all we will see our Lord once again. As our brother Paul wrote, "To be absent from the body is to be present with the Lord." I really can't fathom what this will be like but we will soon find out. Remember the Lord, Peter? Yes I have and will do so until that last stroke of the sword. In some ways I don't think I have to remember the Lord as something in the past because I have always sensed him with us. Even now I sense his presence. I trust that you too feel him there with you. I am concerned for our children and grandchildren but I can only commit them into the hands and care of our Lord. I hope that they go to Britain like they said they felt the Lord wanted them to. Possibly the persecution will not reach them there.

So now I hear the commotion of soldiers outside my cell. I wonder if this means that they are preparing to take me out to the place of execution. But I have perfect peace. I know that you couldn't hear my musings on our life together, most of which has revolved around our Lord and his work, but I trust that the Holy Spirit will have let you sense them.

But soon we will be together again and will be able to reminisce with each other face to face. But until that time, I too say to you, "Remember the Lord."